MW00799532

THE
STAFFORDSHIRE TERRIERS

AMERICAN STAFFORDSHIRE TERRIER
——AND——
STAFFORDSHIRE BULL TERRIER

BY

ANNA KATHERINE NICHOLAS

TS-143

Title page: Ch. Guardstock's Red Atom, Staffordshire Bull Terrier owned by Judi Daniels and Joe LeBlanc; and Ch. Sooner's Big Mac, American Staffordshire Terrier bred by Lois Smith and owned by Olivia Patterson.

The portrayal of canine care products in this book is for instructive value only and does not necessarily constitute the endorsement of the author, the publisher, or the owners of the dogs illustrated in this book.

*This book is dedicated
to all the handsome
Staffordshires and
their enthusiastic, patient
owners*

*The Staffordshire
Terriers: world
renowned dogs.*

© **Copyright 1991 by T.F.H. Publications, Inc.**

Distributed in the UNITED STATES by T.F.H. Publications, Inc., One T.F.H. Plaza, Neptune City, NJ 07753; in CANADA to the Pet Trade by H & L Pet Supplies Inc., 27 Kingston Crescent, Kitchener, Ontario N2B 2T6; Rolf C. Hagen Ltd., 3225 Sartelon Street, Montreal 382 Quebec; in CANADA to the Book Trade by Macmillan of Canada (A Division of Canada Publishing Corporation), 164 Commander Boulevard, Agincourt, Ontario M1S 3C7; in ENGLAND by T.F.H. Publications, The Spinney, Parklands, Portsmouth PO7 6AR; in AUSTRALIA AND THE SOUTH PACIFIC by T.F.H. (Australia) Pty. Ltd., Box 149, Brookvale 2100 N.S.W., Australia; in NEW ZEALAND by Ross Haines & Son, Ltd., 82 D Elizabeth Knox Place, Panmure, Auckland, New Zealand; in the PHILIPPINES by Bio-Research, 5 Lippay Street, San Lorenzo Village, Makati, Rizal; in SOUTH AFRICA by Multipet Pty. Ltd., P.O. Box 35347, Northway, 4065, South Africa. Published by T.F.H. Publications, Inc. Manufactured in the United States of America by T.F.H. Publications, Inc.

Contents

About the Author.. 4

Origin and History of the Bull and Terrier Breeds..............7

The Breeds in the United States..19
Am Staffs in the U.S.A., 19; Call Me Staffs, 19; Cock 'N' Bull, 20; Haus Trevilians, 23; Evergreen, 24; Iron Buck, 26; KirKee, 27; Kodiak, 29; Ledge Rock, 32; Sword and Sorcery (S'N'S), 34; WildWind Farm, 42; Staffordshire Bull Terriers in the U.S.A., 44; Barker's, 44; Blue Steel, 44; Buckland, 45; Bullseye, 46; Davenhill, 51; Doc's, 53; Dragonquest-Nazan, 54; Normandie, 54; Sans Tache, 56; Starzend, 58; Steinstaff, 60; Win-R, 64; Val Verde, 65

The Breeds in Australia and New Zealand 69
Deadgame, 72; Evastaff, 75; Tuskalear, 76

Staffordshire Bull Terriers in Great Britain 77
Mr. and Mrs. R. Austin, 80; Mr. T.A. Norton, 80; Sheila and Peter Wall, 81; Tondoo, 88

Staffordshire Bull Terriers in Canada 91
Coalminer, 91

Staffordshire Terrier Breed Standards 95
Standard for the American Staffordshire Terrier, 95; Standard for the Staffordshire Bull Terrier, 97; British Standard for the Staffordshire Bull Terrier, 1935, 100; British Standard for the Staffordshire Bull Terrier, 102

Colors and Movement: Staffordshire Bull Terrier
By John H. Martin, D.V.M. 105
Action in the Staffordshire Bull Terrier, 106

The Purchase of Your Staffordshire....................................109
Owning a Staffordshire, 122; American Staffordshire Owners Talk of Their Breed, 125

The Care of Your Staffordshire Puppy...........................135
Joining the Family, 141; Socializing and Training, 142; Feeding Your Dog, 147; All Dogs Need to Chew, 150

The Making of a Show Dog 157
General Considerations, 157; Match Shows, 160; Point Shows, 161; Junior Showmanship Competition, 174; Pre-Show Preparations, 178; Enjoying the Dog Show, 183

Your Staffordshire and Obedience 191
Working Your Stafford in Obedience, By Faith Steinman, 193

Breeding Your Staffordshire 199
The Brood Bitch, 202; The Stud Dog, 208; Pregnancy, Whelping, and the Litter, 220; A Caution, 231;

Traveling with Your Staffordshire 233

A Gallery of Historical Photos...240

Index...249

As showmen, companions, and all-around working dogs, the Staffordshire Terriers are undefeatable.

About the Author

Miss Anna Katherine Nicholas, dog expert with over 60 years experience, is a multiple award winner (including Best Technical Book of the Year) for her indefatigable writing proliferation.

Since early childhood, Anna Katherine Nicholas has been involved with dogs. Her first pets were a Boston Terrier, an Airedale, and a German Shepherd Dog. Then, in 1925, came the first of the Pekingese, a gift from a friend who raised them. Now her home is shared with two Miniature Poodles and numerous Beagles.

Miss Nicholas is best known throughout the Dog Fancy as a writer and as a judge. Her first magazine article, published in *Dog News* magazine around 1930, was about Pekingese, and this was followed by a widely acclaimed breed column, "Peeking at the Pekingese," which appeared for at least two decades, originally in *Dogdom*, then, following the demise of that publication, in *Popular Dogs*. During the 1940s she was a Boxer columnist for *Pure-Bred Dogs/American Kennel Gazette* and for *Boxer Briefs*. More recently many of her articles, geared to interest fanciers of every breed, have appeared in *Popular Dogs, Pure-Bred Dogs/American Kennel Gazette, Show Dogs, Dog Fancy, The World of the Working Dog*, and in both Canadian publications, *The Dog Fancier* and *Dogs in Canada*. Her *Dog World* column, "Here, There and Every-

where," was the Dog Writers' Association of America winner of the Best Series in a Dog Magazine Award for 1979. Another feature article of hers, "Faster Is Not Better," published in *Canine Chronicle*, received Honorable Mention on another occasion.

In 1970 Miss Nicholas won the Dog Writers' Association Award for the Best Technical Book of the Year with her *Nicholas Guide to Dog Judging*. In 1979 the revision of this book again won this award, the first time ever that a revision has been so honored by this organization. Other important dog writer awards which Miss Nicholas has gained over the years have been the Gaines "Fido" and the *Kennel Review* "Winkies," these both on two occasions and each in the Dog Writer of the Year category.

It was during the 1930s that Miss Nicholas's first book, *The Pekingese*, appeared in print, published by the Judy Publishing Company. This book, and its second edition, sold out quickly and is now a collector's item, as is *The Skye Terrier Book* which was published during the 1960s by the Skye Terrier Club of America.

During recent years, Miss Nicholas has been writing

books consistently for T.F.H. These include *Successful Dog Show Exhibiting, The Book of the Rottweiler, The Book of the Poodle, The Book of the Labrador Retriever, The Book of the English Springer Spaniel, The Book of the Golden Retriever, The Book of the German Shepherd Dog, The Book of the Shetland Sheepdog, The Book of the Miniature Schnauzer, The World of Doberman Pinschers,* and *The World of Rottweilers.* Plus, in another T.F.H. series, *The Maltese, The Keeshond, The Chow Chow, The Poodle, The Boxer, The Beagle, The Basset Hound, The Dachshund* (the latter three co-authored with Marcia A. Foy), *The German Pointer, The Collie, The Weimaraner, The Great Dane, The Dalmatian, The Pekingese, The Samoyed,* and *The Fox Terrier.* In the KW series she has done *Rottweilers, Weimaraners, Jack Russell Terriers, Finnish Spitz, French Bulldogs, Staffordshire Bull Terriers, American Staffordshire Terriers* and *Norwegian Elkhounds.* And she has written American chapters for two popular English books purchased and published in the United States by T.F.H., *The Staffordshire Bull Terrier* and *The Jack Russell Terrier.*

Miss Nicholas's association with T.F.H. began in the early 1970s when she co-authored for them five books with Joan Brearley: *The Wonderful World of Beagles and Beagling* (also honored by the Dog Writers Association), *This is the Bichon Frise, The Book of the Pekingese, The Book of the Boxer,* and

This is the Skye Terrier.

Among Miss Nicholas's up and coming additions to dog literature are two volumes on the Rottweiler and Shar-Pei, books sure to be the most definitive and complete texts ever published.

Since 1934 Miss Nicholas has been a popular dog show judge, officiating at prestigious events throughout the United States and Canada. She is presently approved for all Hounds, all Terriers, all Toys and all Non-Sporting; plus all Pointers, English and Gordon Setters, Vizslas, Weimaraners, and Wirehaired Pointing Griffons in the Sporting Group and Boxers and Dobermans in Working. In 1970 she became only the third woman ever to have judged Best in Show at the famous Westminster Kennel Club event at Madison Square Garden in New York City, where she has officiated as well on some sixteen other occasions over the years. She has also officiated at such events as Santa Barbara, Chicago International, Morris and Essex, Trenton, Westchester, etc., in the United States; the Sportsman's and the Metropolitan among numerous others in Canada; and Specialty shows in several dozen breeds in both countries. She has judged in almost every one of the United States and in four of the Canadian Provinces. Her dislike of air travel has caused her to refrain from acceptance of the constant invitations to officiate in other parts of the world.

Esteemed as one of the best, Miss Nicholas has judged dogs since 1934.

This is Ch. Guardstock's Red Atom, assuredly a credit to both Judi Daniels and Joe LeBlanc.

Origin and History of the Bull and Terrier Breeds

The Staffordshire Terriers trace their roots to the old Bull and Terrier crosses of the 1800s or possibly even earlier.

Although official recognition by both the Kennel Club of Great Britain and the American Kennel Club did not come to the Staffordshire Terrier until the mid-1930s, the ancestry of these dogs can be traced back at least as far as the beginning of the nineteenth century. The Staffordshire, in common with the Bull Terrier and with, actually, the Boston Terrier, descends from the old Bull and Terrier cross which had been seen both in Britain and in the United States since the 1800s or possibly even earlier.

Bull and Terrier dogs first became known in England during the early 1800s, when "bulldogs" were most carefully bred for the express purpose of baiting bulls. There is a vast difference between dogs then known as "bulldogs" and our modern breed of that name, the ones of the 1800s having been dogs of agility; they were straight-legged, sometimes with a longish muzzle, and they often had long rat-like tails. We

have read that their actual resemblance, with the exception of head properties, was far closer to those dogs later known as American Staffordshire Terriers than it was to those we now call Bulldogs.

With this early "bulldog," a terrier cross was introduced: probably the Black and Tan Terrier (progenitor of the Manchester Terrier), or a large white dog known as the English Terrier. It has also been suggested that Fox Terriers might have been introduced as well, due to that breed's exceptional gameness.

It is unfortunate that the exceptional gameness, fearlessness, and hardiness of these Bull and Terrier dogs led to their exploitation as fighting dogs in Great Britain and the United States.

The interbreeding of the early "bulldog" and the old English Terrier with whatever other terrier lines may or may not have been included,

Ch. Steeltown's Blue Monday, owned by Dr. Jerry E. Brown and Julianna A. Brown, being handled by Mike Shea.

produced the dogs eventually named Staffordshire Bull Terriers. The dogs of that early period were especially popular with the coal mining and heavy industry workers of the Staffordshire area, thus the name seemed appropriate.

When, in 1835, bullbaiting was outlawed throughout Great Britain, dogfighting moved in to take its place. Then as time progressed, humane societies gained their point, and the cruel activity of dogfighting was legally abolished. This legislation was not completely successful, we gather, as the practice did continue (although somewhat furtively) until police intervention and strict enforcement of the law started to occur in the 1930s.

Many fanciers of the Pit dogs (or Half and Halfs, Bull and Terriers, or Pit Bull Terriers, as they also were known) gave thought to a more legitimate form of competition with their dogs—that of having them compete in the dog *show* ring. Thus, in 1935, the Bull and Terrier received the approval of the Kennel Club of Great Britain and admission to the Stud Book registry for Staffordshire Bull Terriers. A Specialty Club was formed for the advancement and protection of the breed's best interests, and a standard of the breed, describing the desirable character and physical conformation of these dogs was drawn up. The game, courageous, and hardy Bull and

Terrier was started on the road to respectability. Between 1939 and 1970, registrations increased from 350 to more than 2,000. The Staffordshire has held its popularity well in England.

Toward the end of the Civil War, British workers from financially troubled and depressed industrial areas in their own country came to the United States. A number of them brought their Bull and Terrier dogs, the breeding of which was continued under such names as the American Bull Terrier, Yankee Terrier, and Pit Bull Terrier. These dogs became recognized by the United Kennel Club, which still sponsors them today, and which conducts a registry for the breed. The Pit Bull Terrier breed, its registry, and the United Kennel Club are not recognized by the American Kennel Club.

After arriving in the United States, Bull and Terrier owners continued to have their dogs engage in dogfights. Despite that, many of them used their dogs as companions and playmates for children, and for working purposes when they settled in what many times were quite desolate areas. These dogs were appreciated for their devotion to people and for their reliability, which was fortunate for the future of the breed.

Pit fighting was outlawed in the United States too, long before now. As in England, those with concern for animals

and hatred of cruelty have pressed for outlawing and entirely eliminating this activity. It would seem that with all the interests and pleasure this modern world has to offer, human beings could find *many* more constructive and engrossing diversions other than watching dogs tear each other apart. The practice is cruel, inhumane, and unnecessary. To put the kindest possible light on its followers,

Ch. Bullseye Red Renegade winning one of his many Bests of Breed, this time from Edith Izant. J. Zane Smith is owner-handling this renowned Staffordshire Bull Terrier.

These folks and their dogs are gathered for the very first rally of the Staffordshire Bull Terrier Club of the US, which was held at the Rants' on February 4, 1968. The enthusiastic fanciers include Larry and Lilian Rant, Judy Venable, Dan Venable, Steve Stowe, Betty Crowther, Jack and Sharon Harrison, and Mrs. Liversidge.

we once read that possibly it was not cruelty that prompted so many to revel in the practice of pitting dog against dog, but rather a streak of admiration for the strength, agility, and fearlessness of these animals. Looking at this subject any way one likes, it has left a hard-to-overcome stigma on the dogs of Bull and Terrier descent. No matter how many good and courageous acts these dogs perform, no matter how frequently their loyalty and intelligence is demonstrated, no matter how many lives they help to save and children they tend and adore, there are still those people who will continue to feel that they are dangerous and unreliable. A Bull and Terrier dog wants nothing more than to please his master. Thus, the conduct of the dogs is largely dependent on the beliefs, conduct, and proper upbringing with which they

are—or are not—raised. When ferocity is demanded, wanted, and expected by the human, the dog trains easily to comply. If, on the other hand, the dog's good qualities are the ones encouraged, the Bull and Terrier stands right high on the list of thoroughly desirable, reliable, loving, amusing, intelligent, and friendly canines.

It is now more than half a century since Staffordshire Terriers were recognized by the Kennel Club of Great Britain and the American Kennel Club. (These events took place in 1936.) In the United States, too, a strong and active Specialty Club was promptly organized—the Staffordshire Terrier Club of America. This organization was accepted in membership to the AKC in 1940. Meanwhile, a standard for the breed was drawn up, and the breeding and showing of Staffordshires took on an enthusiastic following. Early Specialty Shows in America, held during the 1940s, were sponsored by the Staffordshire Club in conjunction with the International Kennel Club of Chicago. They usually gathered entries of at least 50 of the breed.

Staffordshire Terriers were the nineteenth Terrier breed to be officially approved by the AKC. The breed's first AKC registration, in 1936, was Wheeler's Black Dinah. In 1937, Champion Maher's Captain D became the first Staffordshire Terrier to become an American Kennel Club Champion of Record.

A very famous name in Staffordshire history of the mid-1900s (prior to the separation of Staffordshires into two breeds during the 1970s)

was the great Champion X-Pert Brindle Biff, a very outstanding winner and a dog who left a legacy of an imposing number of champions who helped carry their sire's quality to future generations. Biff was owned by his breeder Clifford A. Ormsby. Other well-known Staffordshires of the mid-1900s included Champion Topsy's Ghost; Champion X-Pert Pedro Escopeta, owned by Dr. Carroll A. Roll; a son of Escopeta, Champion Rip Rock Irish Mike, bred and owned by Oscar and Kathleen Marusich; Champion Rip Rock Golden Rock (another son of Escopeta), bred by Mr. and Mrs. Marusich and owned by Mrs. Dean D. Howard; the daughter of Clifford Ormsby's Brindle Biff, Champion Glamour Girl; and Champion Rip Rock Silver Cavalier, owned by Clifford

Ch. Steeltown's Blue Monday, taking a Terrier Group Second. Mike Shea handling this Am Staff for owners, Cock 'N' Bull Kennels, Bloomington, CA.

Ch. Sooner's Big Mac. By Ch. Sooner's Ranger el Cajohn ex Merrily Mimi of Hiccup Hill. This Am Staff, bred by Lois Smith and owned by Olivia Patterson, is a Top Producer.

Marusich. All were well known in the show rings.

As the years progressed, it became increasingly evident that there was considerable difference developing between Staffordshire Bull Terriers bred in the United States from American stock and those from or bred from British and Australian stock. This was making for a very wide deviation of type in the breed. The solution was *two separate breeds*. So it was that on January 1, 1972, the American Staffordshire Terrier replaced the Staffordshire Terrier; on October 1, 1974, the "new" breed, Staffordshire Bull Terrier, with a standard of its own, was admitted to the AKC Stud Book. (Dog show classification in the Terrier Group was provided, starting on March 5, 1975.)

As separate breeds, the American Staffordshire Terrier and Staffordshire Bull Terrier have prospered. The American Staffordshire people retained the standard for Staffordshires, feeling it to be an applicable description of their dogs.

Staffordshire Bull Terrier fanciers chose a standard which more accurately described the Staffordshire Bull.

The Stafford Bull is a shorter legged, chunkier dog who weighs in at 24 to 34 pounds and measures between 14 and 16 inches in height at the withers. The Am Staff is longer legged and in this regard is a taller dog, although still solid, muscular, and well balanced. His height ranges from 18 to 19 inches at the withers; bitches measure between 17 to 18 inches in height.

The type differences between the two breeds are becoming increasingly more substantial. Obviously, the talents of the breeders in *both* cases are being turned to the benefit of the dogs, and it is usually a pulse-quickening experience to watch them in the rings at the important shows where many turn out to compete against one another.

Who could possibly write a book about American Staffordshires without paying tribute to such dedicated breeders as the owners and Staffs of such kennels as Ruffian, X-Pert, Gallant, Tryarr, and the many others who have contributed to quality in the breed? Nor could such a book be written without tribute to that superb dog who made so many fanciers of other breeds "Am Staff conscious," Champion Ruffian Red Rock of Har-Wyn. Born in 1972, bred by Mrs. W. O. Harper, and handled by Houston Clark, this

magnificent dog was owned by Rudolph V. and Nancy Esteves at Kansas City, Missouri. He was a son of the famous Champion Ruffian Sky Bolt of Har-Wyn and Ruffian Pink Lady of Har-Wyn.

Ruffian Red Rock belonged to a family of exceptionally distinguished Am Staffs, and he was a credit to them all! His sire, Champion Ruffian Sky Bolt of Har-Wyn, was the sire of many additional notable Am Staffs, including Champion Tryarr Diamondback Redbolt, who has made his own presence strongly felt in the show ring and as a stud dog. My first look

Ch. Sooner's Dr. Pepper at age nine months. One of the quality Am Staffs at Sooner Kennels. Owner, Elmer Perkins.

13

Ch. WildWind's Amy Tequila, daughter of Ch. Sooner True Grit of Rhody ex Ch. Tex-Rock Queen of Diamonds. Another memorable Am Staff bitch owned by this kennel, WildWinds, belonging to Chet and Lauraine Rodgers.

at Red Rock in the ring at a dog show on one of the southern circuits will never be forgotten. Obviously, others felt as I did about him, for his list of successes is a lengthy one and under a diversified assortment of dog show authorities.

Another great dog handled by Houston Clark was Mr. and Mrs. Levon C. Register's Champion Crusader's Gay Blade. He was born in March 1970 by Champion Tiger Crusader II ex Crusader's Cinderella and bred by Mrs.

I. N. Stinson. Another of the Clarks' "charges" was Champion Gallant Pistol Pete, belonging to E. D. Ringold, Decatur, Michigan. This noted dog was son of Champion Gallant Kimbo R ex Rebel's Jess R.

The Staffordshire Terrier Club of America was approved for membership in the AKC in 1940. It continues today, fostering the best interests of the American Staffordshire Terrier and publishing a newsletter of value and importance to the breed. Among the directors of this club are Charles Lloyd, President, and board members I. Lehr Brisbin, Vice President and AKC delegates, Jacqueline Fraser, Vice President; and Al Amisano, Secretary-treasurer.

S.B.T.C.I. sponsors successful annual Specialty shows and other activities of interest and value to owners of this breed.

The Staffordshire Bull Terrier attained full maturity as a breed in the United States when, on October 1, 1974, he was admitted to registration in the AKC, followed by show classification as a member of the Terrier Group on March 5 of the following year.

Since that time, much has been accomplished in the acceptance, interest, and success of these lovely dogs! True, Staffordshires have been known over many decades in the United States, and Staffordshire Terriers were first registered with AKC in the

mid-1930s. It was decided that too many differences in the dogs had developed over the years for all of them to exist under the single heading of Staffordshire Terriers. Thus, the Staffordshire best known in the United States became the American Staffordshire Terrier in 1972; in 1974, official recognition was given to the Staffordshire Bull Terrier.

Specialty Match Shows arranged by the Stafford fancy. It took the author no time at all to fall in love with Claude Williams's Gamecock Another Brinsley, who was consistently seen in the Miscellaneous ring under the expert handling of Damara Bolte. It is appropriate that this dog became a champion when regular classification became effective.

Prior to their classification into two breeds, Staffordshire Bull Terriers were consigned to the Miscellaneous Class, with breeders working to promote a knowledge of the type of differences between the "new" breed and the former one, and to make the American dog public conscious of the little Staffords as exemplary family and companion dogs.

Some handsome future champions were widely campaigned, not only in the Miscellaneous Classes at all-breed dog shows, but at

We believe he was the first in the country, surely the first in the East, to win a Group placement (which he did under Canadian Terrier breeder-judge, James G. Reynolds).

1975 saw 15 Staffords attain championship honors, awarded in the nine months of competition following the breed's inclusion in the Terrier Group. The first of these was the famous Champion Northwark Becky Sharpe, an importation from Australia, who was representative of Marion Forester's Loggerhead

Aust. Ch. Deadgame Buck Rogers, by Ch. Loggerhead Penkridge ex Deadgame Carmine Chaos, was bred by Deadgame Staffordshires and is owned by Ray and Sandra Willis, New South Wales, Australia. A magnificent specimen of black type, noted for his athletic ability. A.C.C. winner at the New South Wales British Terrier Show.

15

Ch. Silverzend Satan, the SBT Club of America's Top Dog for 1975, '76, and '77, was bred by Dana and Jenny Merritt of Trugrip Kennels. Trugrip also bred the Top Dog and Top Bitch for 1983.

Kennels. Becky Sharpe, owned by Judi and Bill Daniels of Starzend Kennels, produced eight champions.

Following Becky Sharpe during the same year one finds Champion Tinkinswood Imperial, Champion Gamecock Another Brinsley Lad, Champion Gamecock Winter Shadow, Champion Y-Ram Lad Alice, Champion Red Polly of Salken, Champion Gamecock Collector's Item, Champion Silverzend Satan (who became the Staffordshire Bull Terrier Club of America's Top Dog for three consecutive years, 1975-1977), Champion Constable's Billy Club of Silverlake, Champion Millgarth Powerpack, C.D., Champion Starzend Faultless, Champion Silverlake Gemstock, Champion Gamecock Night Must Fall, Champion Ragtime Bombasto, and Champion Estrella's Valhalla Estrallita, C.D. (Notes of special interest on these first champions are that two of them also completed C.D. titles that year.)

Two dozen Staffords became champions during 1976, the breed's first full year of competition. They were: Champion Conqueror's Caesar, Champion Conqueror's Contessa, Champion Chainmaker Brazen Bomber, Champion Trugrip Jezebel, Champion Blackcountry Kipper, Champion Gamecock Dark Image, Champion Starzend Deacon, Champion Texsraff Royal Jester,

Champion Gamecock Hatchetman, Champion Piltdown Red Contessa, Champion Silverlake Dreadnought, Champion Trugrip Horatio Hornblower, Champion Gamecock The Great White Hope, Champion Kavalier's Lord Jeff, Champion Chainmaker Amour Augusta, Champion Trugrip Pendragon Red, Champion Wystall Warlock, Champion Starzend Headliner, Champion Kingsblood Royal Val, Champion Nutmeg Force Majeure, Champion Starzend Isadora, Champion Kalliope's Faust, Champion Starzend Fred Again, and Champion Silverlake Gypsy Queen.

The number of champions has continued to increase year after year, a healthy sign of continued enthusiasm and interest in the breed.

Since 1969, Trugrip Kennels, owned by Dana and Jenny Merritt, have been producing outstanding Staffords of superior quality. The Trugrip foundation bitch was Champion Constable's Billy Club of Silverlake, and the kennel's record stands at around two dozen homebred champions. In addition to being the breeder of Champion Silverzend Satan (from the Merritt's Billy Club), Trugrip also bred the Top Dog and Top Bitch in 1983, not to mention the success with which its Staffords have met in Group competition.

No longer active, but a great breed force during earlier times, especially in the East,

The SBT Club of S. Indiana supported entry on September 15, 1984, was won by Ch. Lochness Ravoon Buster (left); Best of Opposite Sex went to his daughter Masebo's Awesome Alice (right). Mrs. Judi Daniels is the judge. Paul R. Hunt and J. David Massey are the handlers.

was Piltdown Kennels at Park Ridge, New Jersey, owned by Edward and Stella Rowland. The Piltdown foundation Stafford was an imported dog, American and Canadian Champion Millgarth Powerpack, C.D., one of the 1975 United States champions and the first of his breed to attain *both* a conformation and obedience title. Brought from England to America by the Rowlands, he was a son of Salken Resolute ex Craftwood Fancy and sired numerous champions. It was Mr. and Mrs. Rowland who also imported and sold Champion Red Polly of Salken. Purchased by Mr. and Mrs. John Jefferies, Polly became a winner and

Ch. Sans Tache's El Chivato at age 10 months was Best of Winners at the AKC Centennial in 1984. Sired by England's Top Staffordshire Bull Terrier for 1981, Ch. Peg's Bolton Trip ex Kenwunn Supreme, Sans Tache is owned by Joe LeBlanc.

17

WildWind's Arabian Knight, male Am Staff, age 20 months, by Ch. Sooner's True Grit of Rhodys ex Ch. Tex-Rock Queen of Diamonds. Owners, Chet and Lauraine Rodgers.

producer of note.

Also one of the very active eastern breed pioneers was Mrs. Jeanne Pierrette Dross, who owned Normandie Staffords at Albany, New York. Mrs. Dross was the owner of a little dog who did much to make this author love the breed—Champion Piltdown Keltic Druid. His affectionate personality and manner certainly made friends for him and for the breed in the East. "Patton," as he was known, was a son of English, American, Canadian, and Mexican Champion Reetun's Lord Jim ex Piltdown St. Eve. His show career started at age six months in August 1978 at a large Specialty Match where he accounted for Best Puppy. Mrs. Dross has bred several champions and has been a very keen supporter of shows.

The Staffordshire Bull Terrier Club is an active and progressive organization. *Staff Status* is a splendid tri-annual publication of the Staffordshire Bull Terrier Club of America which every Stafford fancier should read, as it is filled with interesting, helpful information, many photos, and all the latest news about the breed.

We are pleased to bring you stories of some of America's leading kennels of both American Staffordshire Terriers and Staffordshire Bull Terriers. We feel that these kennel stories are of utmost importance in compiling a breed history, as they provide accurate, up-to-date particulars on the dogs and the people who have contributed well to the progress of these breeds.

The Breeds in the United States

AM STAFFS IN THE U.S.A.

CALL ME STAFFS

Call Me Staffs Kennels, located at Black Mountain, North Carolina, belong to Kaye M. Roberts, a very dedicated fancier of the American Staffordshire Terrier.

The leading lady at this establishment is a truly gorgeous bitch, Champion Tara's Muddi Fields Forever, daughter of Champion Sindelar's Doctor Mudd (who is also sire of the noted dog, Champion Tara's Doc Holliday) ex Champion Tryarr Strawberry Fields (by Champion Ruffian Red Rock of Har-Wyn). Muddi is co-owned by Kaye and Stacie Lee Brown, Muddi's junior showmanship handler.

Although shown on an extremely limited basis in 1985 and 1986, Muddi distinguished herself by becoming the No. 5 American Staffordshire Terrier.

In her 36 ventures into the show ring during 1985 and through June 1986, Muddi's total wins are as follows: 22 times Best of Breed; 10 times

Ch. Cal! Me Rhett Butler, born in March, 1985, taking Best of Winners at Old Dominion K.C. to complete his title at age 13 months. Breeder-owner, Kay M. Roberts, Call Me Staffs.

19

Best of Opposite Sex; twice Group Third; and three times Group Fourth. Peter Baines, Muddi's professional handler, is anxious to campaign her on a full-time basis, but Muddi has a more important job: that of being the Roberts's house pet and full-time companion. As Mrs. Roberts says, "The fact is that in the few times we were able to part with her for her to be shown, she has done so well that it is truly a credit to her quality and ability."

To date, Muddi has whelped just one litter, but a notable one. Bred to Champion Tara's Doc Holliday, her half brother (also by Champion Sindelar's Doctor Mudd), she produced a litter which included Champion Call Me Katie Scarlet , who finished at age 12 months and is owned by Mrs. Hugh C. Brown, Jr., and Champion Call Me Rhett Butler, who has remained with Mrs. Roberts and who finished at age 13

months.

Muddi, along with two of her offspring, are competing in obedience matches in preparation for trials. Two other puppies are also being trained for tracking.

COCK 'N' BULL

Cock 'N' Bull Kennels are located at Bloomington, California, where they are co-owned by Dr. Jerry E. Brown and Julianna A. Brown. Although primarily involved with American Staffordshires, the Browns are actually great enthusiasts of *all* Staffordshires. As well as owning Am Staffs, the Browns own representatives of the Pit Bulls and, I believe, a Stafford or two.

Pride of place in this kennel goes to the magnificent Am Staff dog, Champion Steeltown's Blue Monday who, handled by Mike Shea, has earned a formidable list of wins coast to coast, one of his most recent being Best of Breed at 1987's Westminster. During his career as a "special," Blue Monday has amassed a formidable number of Bests of Breed, multiple Best Terrier awards, and about 50 additional Group placements.

Blue Monday started his show career at age four months when he took Best Puppy in Match at a Bull Breed Specialty. At nine months he began obedience work, and at 15 months he had completed his conformation championship with four "majors" and Best of Breed wins from the classes.

Ch. Evergreen's Midnight Lace completed title in four straight shows. By Ch. White Rock Jet Bomber ex Ch. Evergreen Earth Angel, she is homebred and owned by Jim and Carolyn Brown, Evergreen Kennels.

When just over two years of age, his Bests of Breed stood at 50 and his Group placements numbered around 20. His career has continued with this same type of success.

Blue Monday's pedigree is one of particular interest, going back to some of the truly great Am Staffs who helped establish the breed in the winners circle here. His sire, Champion White Rock Dusty of Steeltown, is by Champion White Rock Jet Bomber (Champion Ruffian Hercules of Har-Wyn-Champion Archer's Muneca Dulsie De G's, C.D.) ex Champion Patton's White Rock Penny (White Rock Grover-Champion Patton's Texas Belle Lucy).

A true patriot and a splendid Am Staff, Ch. Steeltown's Blue Monday is one from the Cock 'N' Bull Kennels, owned by Dr. and Mrs. J. Brown.

Ch. White Rock Dusty of Steeltown, handled by Julianna A. Brown for Cock 'N' Bull Kennels, Bloomington, CA, here taking Best of Breed from the classes on the way to championship.

Blue Monday's dam is Deno's Diamond of Steeltown. Diamond was sired by Champion Diamond's Paladin (Champion Tryarr Diamondback Redbolt-Champion Tryarr Blue Diamond) from Champion Circe Von Brown (a descendant of Sooner and Patton breeding).

With so solid a background of producers, Blue Monday is carrying on as one would expect by producing some lovely young Staffs in his own right.

Blue Monday and the Browns are among the Am Staffs and their owners who are working with the Humane Society's Animal Facilitated Therapy Program. His owners feel that Blue Monday's participation as a therapy dog is his finest achievement.

Ch. Steeltown's Blue Monday, taking Best of Breed, owned by Cock 'N' Bull Kennels. Photo by Missy Yuhl.

BEST OF BREED OR VARIETY

MISSY PHOTO

Three of the handsome young American Staffs at Haus Trevilians Kennels, owned by Doug Loving, of Richmond, VA.

HAUS TREVILIANS

The Haus Trevilians Kennel was established in 1976 by Douglas K. Loving of Richmond, Virginia, initially breeding Rottweilers. Then Doug Loving was introduced to American Staffordshires by his handler, Sid Lamont, and by Lenna Hanna, owner of S'N'S Staffs. The result was that since 1985 the kennel has been concentrating on the Am Staff.

Doug's first Staff was S'N'S Ogre Easy, a most excellent show dog who has been doing well in the U.S. and Canada. At present, he is building up an imposing list of Best of Breed awards and Group placements. Most of all, however, Doug loves this splendid dog's easy-going, friendly attitude, as well as his protective nature. "Crunch," as he is known, has proven himself to be safe with other dogs and is not a fighter. Bred by John Sparks and Lenna Hanna, he is co-owned by Douglas Loving, Haus Trevilians, and Lenna Hanna. Born April 11, 1983, Crunch is by Champion Sooner's Oklahoma Pride from Sooner's Fudge Ripple.

It is required that all bitches brought to Ogre Easy for stud service be of sound temperament, which must be proven by the bitch passing a temperament test. Crunch stands at stud only to AKC registered bitches, and is *not* available to United Kennel Club Pit Bulls or dual-registered AKC/UKC bitches.

Doug Loving's background in dogs has been primarily in Schutzhund work, and he is a firm believer that all dogs should be capable of performing the tasks for which they were bred. He has worked as a wrangler for Metro Goldwyn Mayer Studios and is currently a consultant with the Virginia State Police Department Canine Program.

Ch. Evergreen's Chicago Bear, a tightly bred "Ruffian" dog, is widely admired for his square head with short muzzle and distinct stop; well-muscled short-coupled body. By Ch. Diamond Ringmaster of Evergreen ex Ch. Rocky Mt. Tosca, he is a homebred born September, 1983, bred and owned by Jim and Carolyn Brown.

EVERGREEN

Evergreen American Staffordshire Terriers, at Chicago, Illinois, are in existence because their owners, Jim and Carolyn Brown, truly enjoy Am Staffs, appreciate and love their dogs, and wish to improve the breed. Evergreen American Staffordshires are primarily Ruffian-linebred dogs. Very special attention has been given to them to foster a most congenial personality along with a distinctly conformed, strongly built body. The Browns have met with considerable success in both conformation and obedience rings, and they encourage other Am Staff fanciers to likewise pursue success in both types of competition.

The wonderful producing bitch, Wheezer's Shady Lady, was born in August 1978. Her sire, Champion Mount Shires I'm A Wheezer, is a son of Champion Topstaff Tony The Tiger (by Champion Ruffian Hercules of Har-Wyn-Willynwood Ogre's Angel) from Champion Ruffian Lady of Har-Wyn. Shady Lady is from a bitch called Merle (by Heathcliffe, C.D.X., from Heather's Brindle, C.D.X.) who was of obedience stock. Bred on several occasions to Champion Tryarr Diamondback Redbolt (Champion Ruffian Sky Bolt of Har-Wyn-Topstaff Willywood Goldy), Shady Lady produced, among others, American and Canadian Champion Evergreen's Demon Seed,

C.D., well-known Terrier Group-winning and -placing campaigner. She also is the dam of Champion Evergreen Apache Belle, another Terrier Group winner who is distinguished as the *third* bitch of this breed so honored.

Shady Lady produced numerous other champions, all adding up to make her a Top Producer as well as Winner of the Brood Bitch class of the 1982 National. The well-built body and tremendous personality for which she is famous are clearly recognizable through five generations of her descendants. She plays a very strong part in the Evergreen breeding program.

Two other famous Am Staffs from this kennel include Champion Evergreen's Earth Angel (Champion Tryarr Diamondback Redbolt-Champion Evergreen's Sundancer) and her dam (Sundancer) who is by Redbolt ex Shady Lady. These two girls make up the famous Best in Show-winning brace in whom the Browns take pride. Angel is also the dam of a smashing first litter of five, all of whom look to be destined for championship honors and at least several for obedience degrees.

Champion Evergreen's Chicago Bear, so named as some of the members of the Chicago Bears are among his friends, is a wondrous star at Evergreen. He is by Champion Diamond Ringmaster of Evergreen (Champion Diamond Paladin-Champion Tryarr Diamonds Are Forever) ex Champion Rocky Mountain

Ch. Evergreen's Sundancer who, with her daughter, "Angel," makes up the famous Best in Show Winning Brace of Am Staffs bred and owned by Jim and Carolyn Brown, Evergreen Kennels.

Tosca (Champion Titan's Roho Grande-Champion Rocky Mountain Ogre's Runnaway), making him a product of very tight Ruffian breeding. He is proving a dominant sire, reproducing his many assets in his offspring, and he is a dog who impresses the judges.

IRON BUCK

Iron Buck Staffordshire Terriers, owned by James and Barbara Wheat, are located at Melrose Park, Illinois.

This is the home of Champion Iron Buck's Painted Horse, born August 8, 1980, who finished his championship out of the puppy class, owner-handled, at age eleven months. He is still gaining honors with consistency.

Painted Horse has competed at all of the independent National Specialties through 1985. His first award was won on October 16, 1982 at the Chicago Specialty, where he was judged Best of Opposite Sex. This Specialty was judged by Florise Hogan. At the fourth independent National Specialty, held in California, he was awarded Best of Breed by Mr. Nigel Desmond, winning this honor over an entry of 119 dogs.

Between 1981 and 1985, Painted Horse earned 22 Terrier Group placements. He was in the Top Ten American Staffordshires in 1984 and 1985, and he was the second Top Producer in 1984. History will record him to be one of the "greats."

Then there is Champion Iron

Ch. Iron Buck's Painted Horse, outstanding winning American Staffordshire Terrier bred and owned by James Wheat, Melrose Park, IL. A son of Buck's Iron Spike Jo ex Magnum's Brandy Lady. Painted Horse was born August 8, 1980. Pictured here with his handler Mae Piske.

A popular and widely admired winning Am Staff of the late 1970s, Ch. Mari-Don Kirkee Battery, born June, 1975. The black brindle and white Kirk is 20 inches tall at the withers and weighs in at 68 pounds. Owned by Wayne M. Chariff, Binghamton, NY. Kirk here is proving his show quality by winning Best of Breed at Westchester K.C. in September, 1979.

Buck's Painted Tart, C.D., "all-American dog," born in July 1982. A homebred, she was sired by Painted Horse and is a daughter of Champion Tara's Gingerbread Tart.

Painted Tart finished her championship in conformation by winning her points at five shows. She was a blue ribbon winner in the American-bred class at the 1983 National Specialty.

KIRKEE

Kirkee American Staffordshire Terriers are owned by Wayne M. Chariff and are located at Binghamton,

New York. This very enthusiastic fancier has been associated with the breed over a number of years and has been involved with the ownership and/or breeding of some exceptionally splendid Am Staffs.

The first of the Kirkee Staffs to attract the author's judicial attention was Champion Mari-Don Kirkee Battery, a most impressive dog who, while still in the classes, took Best of Breed at the Bronx County Kennel Club in 1979. "Kirk" is an outstanding example of Am Staff type and quality.

It was through Wayne

Ch. Mar-Jon Kirkee Battery, by Ch. Mar-Don Polly's Black Beau ex Shady Lady of Hiccup Hill was bred by Tom A. Cunningham and is owned by Wayne M. Chariff. Handled here by John C. McCartney to the exciting win of Best of Breed at Montgomery County in October, 1979, under judge R. William Taylor.

event for the Terrier world, Montgomery County.

The following year, John and Kirk started out at Westminster, winning still another important Best of Breed. It was by then quite well established that Kirk was an exceptionally fine Staffordshire Terrier—a fact which he proved not only in the show ring but as a sire as well.

Two weeks after the Westminster win, John received a surprise thank you gift from Wayne. The gift was a beautiful, intelligent, and very affectionate pup who later became Champion Fraja's Thunder Battery. Born October 16, 1979, she was Kirk's daughter from Champion Pepper Ridge Fraja's Thunder. I daresay there is not anyone who regularly attends dog shows in the East who has not met and made friends with Thunder Battery, more familiarly known to us as "Dagmar." She is a magnificent example of what is correct in American Staffordshires, both in personality and in looks. Her friends are legion; and when Dagmar retired, I know that we all felt dog shows would not seem quite the same.

Dagmar went through to her championship with ease, undefeated in her class and winning Reserve Winners Bitch at the National Specialty in Kentucky from the junior puppy class! Then she was put away to grow up prior to her "specials" career. John's impatience to get her back into

Chariff and attendance at the Sand and Sea Kennel Club Dog Show in 1979 that John McCartney began what he refers to as "the great love affair with American Staffordshires that has led to these dogs becoming my favorite breed." As John has handled and lived with many AKC-recognized breeds, his interest in Am Staffs is all the more noteworthy and speaks well of their merit. At their meeting at the Sand and Sea, Wayne Chariff asked John McCartney (whom he had met the previous year at the same show when John had first seen and admired Kirk) if he would show Kirk in the Group that day. John agreed, and he and Kirk became a team whose show successes included Best of Breed a few weeks later at the prestigious Westchester Kennel Club event, and, the following month, Best of Breed at *the*

competition soon took over, and at 16 months she returned to the show ring. This was no mistake, however! Dagmar carried on in Kirk's tradition by becoming the Best of Breed at Westminster upon her return, which made her the youngest Staff to gain this victory. She repeated the win the following year, again taking Best of Breed at Westminster. She also took the breed at Montgomery, as her sire had done.

Dagmar's total show record stands at over 150 times Best of Breed and 30 Group placements, including first place—this in a breed where no other Staff had previously done so in tough eastern Terrier Group competition.

Now that Dagmar has retired, she is thoroughly enjoying life as John McCartney's personal house pet. She has also had two litters. The first consisted of three pups, two of whom are finished and the third one pointed. In the second litter, she had four pups, three of whom are pointed from the puppy class (with one finished at a year's age).

Kirk has also sired such winners as Champion Kirk's Daughter O'The Regiment, from Champion Fraja Maria's Tia Maria, who did some nice winning for Wayne Chariff. She was also handled by John McCartney.

Still another exciting Kirkee winning bitch is Champion Kirkee's Polar Bear of Fraja,

C.D., co-owned by Wayne Chariff and Jacqueline Fraser. Polar Bear was the first bitch in a quarter of a century to have won Best of Breed at the American Staffordshire Club National Specialty. She is by Champion Lucas Cool Hand Luke ex Champion Fraja Maria's Tia Maria.

KODIAK

Kodiak Kennels, owned by Fred J. and Sharon A. Marushak at Quakertown, Pennsylvania, started its interest with American Staffordshire Terriers in 1983 with the purchase of an eight-week-old, white-faced brindle bitch from Art and Wanda Campbell (Aranda Kennels). The Marushaks were looking for a breed which was spirited and hardy enough to live with a household full of Great Danes.

The Marushaks have never regretted their selection. That

Ch. Mari-Don Kirkee Battery in June, 1975, with handler, John C. McCartney and owner, Wayne M. Chariff, as Kirk wins Best of Breed at Westminster in 1980. This dog was a consistent and admired winner of the late 1970s.

Ch. Kodiak's Blaque Jaque, by Ch. Fraja Maria's Ace In The Hole ex Ch. Herk's Kizzy of Fraja. Pictured at age seven months taking Best of Winners at Bald Eagle K.C. Completed title at age 11 months. Born December, 1983. Kodiak Kennels are owned by Fred and Sharon Marushak.

little puppy immediately took over the household, gained the love and respect of all the Great Danes, and stole the hearts of her owners. In addition, she grew into a stunning, vivacious show bitch—Champion Aranda Angelina V. Kodiak. Her sire and dam were Champion Sir Vessa ex Champion Barway Chantilly Lace V. Aranda.

Kodiak's next acquisition, in 1984, was through a rescue of sorts. The Marushaks were contacted by a young couple whose pet had a litter of pups in a No Pets apartment and who were worried that they would be evicted if their landlord heard about the pups. The puppies' mother apparently was quiet enough that the landlord was still unaware of her presence. After meeting with the couple and assuring themselves that the litter had been well bred (Champion Fraja Maria's Ace In The Hole ex Champion Herk's Kizzy of Fraja), raised, and socialized properly, the Marushaks agreed to house the four pups while the young couple continued their search for just the right homes. Of course the Marushaks fell in love with the puppies and saw their potential, so the question was settled by their purchase (for themselves) of the litter. Three of the pups realized the potential foreseen by the Marushaks. They became Champion Kodiak Blaque Jaque, Champion Kodiak's Kare Bear, and Champion Kodiak's The Joker's Wild. The fourth, a bitch, was pointed as a pup but did not mature to their expectations or standards and thus was retired from showing, then spayed.

Kare Bear is in residence at Kodiak Kennels. Kare Bear and Joker's Wild both appeared in a major motion picture, *Angel Heart*, starring Robert DiNiro.

Angelina, the Kodiak foundation bitch, was bred to Dr. Eva Lydick's Texas-bred blue, Champion Byron's Finn McCool, producing Champion Kodiak's Blue Haze; Kodiak's Rhythm in Blue (13 points, both "majors"); Kodiak's Tina Turner Review (8 points, one major); and Kodiak's

Kodiak's Rhythm in Blue, by Ch. Aranda Angelina V. Kodiak ex Ch. Byron's Finn McCool, was born in March, 1985, and is pictured at age six months taking Best of Opposite Sex at Pocono Mountain K.C. Owned by Fred and Sharon Marushak.

Windrider (14 points, both majors).

Kodiak's most recent endeavor, the breeding of Champion Kodiak's Blaque Jaque to Kodiak's Rhythm in Blue, has produced a new cluster of rising stars.

Kodiak Kennels place emphasis in their breeding program on *soundness* of both body and mind. They feel they have achieved these goals thus far in the limited time they have been breeding and will continue to strive toward producing that elusive perfect dog. We wish them the tremendous continued success their dedication, enthusiasm, and true love of the breed deserves.

LEDGE ROCK

Ledge Rock American Staffordshire Terriers are located at Thompson, Ohio, on 20 acres bordering Thompson Ledges. Owners Ernest and Ruth Prehn operate a small hobby/show kennel, which came about as the result of their having acquired one special, high quality dog who really flamed their love for the breed. Their interest in the American Staffordshire Terrier has continued since that time.

The Prehns' first male was Canadian Champion Willynwood Velvet Shadow, C.D. This brindle male was strongly bred on the Gallant-Crusader line. Eventually a brindle and white bitch was

Ch. Ledge Rock's Kopper Korn, by Ch. Titan's Rojo Grande ex Ch. Rowdytown Jazz of Ledge Rock, is a homebred owned by Ernest and Ruth Prehn of Thompson, OH. Here receiving the Best Terrier award from noted terrier expert Ron Krohne. Handler, A. Rehil.

Ch. Ledge Rock's Sweet Potatoe taking Best of Winners at Bucks County in 1986. Owned by Karen Tucker, Pennsburg, PA.

purchased, who was of the Ruffian and Crusader lines (the latter going back four generations in her pedigree).

Ruffian is the dominant line being used in the Prehns' breeding program and one which they find crosses successfully into the Gallant line. The Prehns noted that they have always liked the steady temperament and quiet intelligence of the Gallant dogs, as they do the movement, spirit, and soundness of the Ruffian line.

At Ledge Rock, breeding is done with a long-range program in mind. Its only purpose is to improve what the kennel already has, with an eye toward the future. Thought is given to

what will be done about later breedings as the more imminent ones are planned and accomplished. Much study goes into the pedigrees of both the dog and the bitch; no breeding takes place at this kennel until all puppies from the previous litter are in good homes. Breeding just for the sake of having a litter is *never* undertaken here.

The Prehns prefer to limit the size of their Staff family to two excellent stud dogs and two quality bitches. Of course, their foremost consideration is ideal disposition, which they demand in both their dogs and their bitches.

Champion Ledge Rock's Kopper Korn is the Prehns'

Ch. Sooner's
Black Pepper,
by Ch. Beau
Ringo, U.D.,
ex Ch.
Nugent's
Merry
Midnight,
C.D., was bred
by Lois Smith,
Sooner
American
Staffordshires.

Opposite: Ch.
Sooner's
Lady Love, of
Sword and
Sorcery
Kennels.
Photo courtesy
of Lenna S.
Hanna.

passing along her sweet disposition. Ruth Prehn says that Lucy and her owners, Joe and Joye Lucarelli, have helped in many of the Ledge Rock accomplishments, of which she is appreciative. Lucy is a daughter of the Prehns' Willynwood Shadow and Champion Rowdytown Jazz of Ledge Rock. The old saying of "all it takes is one good bitch" has much truth in it; for Ledge Rock, Lucy is the one.

SWORD AND SORCERY (S'N'S)

Sword and Sorcery American Staffordshire Terriers, sometimes abbreviated as a matter of convenience to 'S'N'S', are owned by Lenna S. Hanna and John Parks, Terlton, Oklahoma. Most of the kennel's dogs are named after fantasy characters. Lenna enjoys the exhibition of the dogs, most of which she does herself. John, on the other hand, prefers working from home base as a trainer and socializer of puppies. He also works with abused dogs who have acquired temperament problems, regardless of their breed. Lenna comments that John can "do surprising things with dogs of spooky temperament, his very gentle nature causing the dogs to respond to him immediately." She has seen him, in a month or less, change many a bucking, unmanageable puppy into an avid showman, which takes a bit of talent. So it is John who does the main

foundation stud dog. This handsome, deep red and white male is linebred with Champion Red Rock of Har-Wyn. "Korny" is a strong stud dog who seems to click well with most lines, endowing his puppies with very good bone and movement.

The Gallant-bred bitch, Champion Ledge Rock's Buckeye Velvet, has provided the outcross in Ledge Rock's breeding activities. This bitch finished at Montgomery in a blaze of glory and won the weight-pulling contest at the November 1984 National Specialty.

Lucarelli Kennels, owned by Joye Lucarelli, has formed a partnership with Ledge Rock and owns the Ledge Rock foundation bitch, Champion Ledge Rock's Lucy in the Sky. She is the Gallant-Ruffian bitch who has added so greatly to the Prehns' kennel and is the strong force in helping the Ledge Rock line. Lucy produces true to the standard and is of outstanding type,

Ch. S'N'S Ogre Easy, or "Crunch" to his friends, is now in the East with Doug Loving by whom he is being campaigned under a co-ownership with Lenna Hanna. Pictured, with Lenna handling, at the Texas Regional Specialty, Corpus Christi, where at age 13 months he took Best of Opposite Sex.

portion of the preliminary training of S'N'S puppies.

While John provides the training, Lenna's forte is her knowledge of anatomy and genetics, gleaned through years of working for a veterinarian and by having majored in biological science at Oklahoma State University, where she spent as many hours as possible on genetic studies.

John and Lenna began in earnest show competition during the early 1970s, starting with the Rottweiler breed. In the mid-1970s, Lenna began traveling with a professional handler, Debbie Goddard, doing so for about five years. She gathered valuable knowledge regarding the presentation of show dogs, plus an introduction to a variety of different breeds. By 1979, the number of Rottweilers in show competition had continued to increase at an almost alarming rate, leaving these two fanciers with the impression that they would find it more satisfying to select a breed less overwhelmingly popular to show.

At about that same time, Lenna's sister's pet Dachshund died of a congenital ailment, leaving behind a most heartbroken owner. This caused Lenna and John to step up their efforts to locate the "ideal" breed, with as few hereditary problems as possible. Lenna had been doing research on Bull Terriers, liking the look of the dogs and leaning heavily toward them as a choice; but John was pushing for American Staffordshires because of their temperament. It was temperament quality and heredity factors that decided the issue in favor of the Staffs.

Lenna's two years of research, with special emphasis on *consistency*, led them to Sooner Kennels and a man named Elmer Parsons. From him Lenna first purchased a pet quality puppy for her sister, this one being Sooner's Ring of Success. She was a daughter of Champion Nugent's Merry Midnight, C.D.; her sire was Champion Sooner's Ranger El Cajohn. Promptly falling in love with "Ring," Lenna and John settled their conflict between Bull Terriers and Staffordshires. Lenna returned to Mr. Parsons's kennel where she purchased Ring's litter sister, "Chantris." This youngster was to become Champion Sooner's Flying Sorceress, who quickly took over as Lenna's constant companion, care dog, bed dog (the only dog in the house ever allowed on a bed), and as an unequaled ambassador of good

will for her breed.

Suddenly it seemed as though Lenna's house was full of Staffs, all of them somehow related to the breeding program of Mr. Parsons or his daughter, Olivia Patterson.

Lenna says, "No history of my breeding program would be complete without giving a great deal of credit to these two people (Elmer Parsons and Olivia Patterson), who bent

Am. and Can. Ch. Sooner's Chocolate Teddy Bear, by Ch. Ruffian Little T of Har-wyn ex Ch. Midnight. Bred by Lois Smith, owned by Olivia and Wayne Patterson. One of the best and most consistent studs. Handled here by Wayne Patterson.

over backwards to provide the help which makes so great a difference in putting a newcomer in a breed off to a successful start. I am forever indebted to them for their cheerful assistance."

to acquire the best of all that the kennel had left. Making this especially notable is the fact the Mr. Parsons's kennel had been established on the old Sooner Kennels which Lois Smith had originally founded.

Ch. Sooner's Shade Midnight Lady with breeder-owner Elmer Parsons.

It is an interesting point in this story that at the period when Lenna became involved with Am Staffs, Mr. Parsons's Sooner Kennels had almost become inactive as breeders. Thus, she and John were able

Thus, S'N'S dogs are actually a continuation of the Sooners and are being bred along the lines established by Lois Smith then carried on by Elmer Parsons and Olivia Patterson.

Lenna explains that she was

Ch. Sooner's Dr. Pepper is one of several American Staffordshire Terriers which Lenna Hanna finished for Elmer Parsons. "Peppy" is a son of Ch. Sooner's Oklahoma Pride ex Hooper's Misti Blud.

originally drawn to Sooner because, of all the breeders she had researched, they were producing Staffs of the type and quality she admired. Sooner excelled in producing dogs with great *clean* fronts, *straight* forelegs, and properly sloping shoulders, pinned *tight* at the withers. In addition, good length and placement of the upper arm assemblage and an excellent front assembly contributed to Sooner's reputation as the producer of dogs with correct toplines and an effortless, smooth, and powerful movement. Sooner dogs were also noted for soundness of body and temperament. To sum it up, Lenna adds, "I like their type, mostly mid-line between the Bull-type and the Terrier-type but leaning toward the latter, with the lovely, classical look of elegance all too rare in this breed."

Following their success with their first show Staff, Champion Sooner's Flying Sorceress, Lenna and John purchased Sooner's Perfectly Demonic, a gorgeous son of Champion Sooner's Our Man Flint ex Sooner's Steamboat Annie. "Aahz," as he was known to his friends, sired only one litter. He was bred to the lovely daughter of Champion Sooner's Ranger El Capitan—Champion Nugent's Merry Midnight, C.D.—their beautiful Chantris. There were four puppies in the litter.

Unfortunately Perfectly Demonic was killed prior to finishing his championship. Lenna tells us that "Pit bull fighters attempted to steal him from his kennel at our place in the city. This dog, unfortunately, was a big friendly cuss, more than willing to take a ride with anyone." As the thieves drove off her

Sooner's Rags to Riches is an addition to the S'N'S stud force owned by John Sparks and Lenna S. Hanna, OK. By Ch. Sooner's Our Man Flint ex Am. and Can. Ch. Halsey's Black Eye Susie, this dog attracted Lenna Hanna's attention by his gorgeous movement. He is already proving himself to be an invaluable sire who will carry on in the Sooner and S'N'S tradition.

property, Lenna saw them leaving with her dog in the back of their car and ran, screaming his name, to the door. The dog heard her and jumped out in an effort to return to her, but was killed crossing the street. A tragedy of course, but considering where this sweet, gentle, and loving dog was being taken, it has to be felt that he is better off. This was the incident that precipitated John and Lenna's move to the country, to a large property where they cannot easily be located and where no Staffs are ever let out without protection-trained Rottweilers.

Around the same time as Aahz was purchased, Lenna acquired Sooner's Fudge Ripple ("Jamie"), a brindle and white bitch bred by Olivia Patterson. Sired by American and Canadian Champion Sooner's Chocolate Teddy Bear ex Champion Don Carlos Blu's Boomerange, Fudge Ripple is the S'N'S foundation bitch. She is one of those very maternal bitches who will produce milk in 24 hours if exposed to crying puppies, so she has not, as yet, had the opportunity to gain title. At the age of five years, she has been bred only twice but has raised four litters for

Lenna, among them a Dachshund litter; so she has been either "bagged up" or out of condition to be shown. She is the dam of Champion S'N'S Ogre Easy, widely known as "Crunch," who was bred by John and Lenna and is now co-owned with Doug Loving. Crunch, whose sire is Champion Sooner's Oklahoma Pride, was named for a fictional character, a vegetarian ogre named "Crunch-no-Bone." Crunch was the gentle giant among his litter mates. The largest, stockiest pup, with a peculiar concern for the runt bitch, he always saw to it that she got to eat first, instead of hogging in like the rest of his siblings. Because of his size and attitude, his name seemed a natural for him.

Crunch made his point show debut at the National Specialty in 1984, in Dallas, Texas, after a successful preview at the fun matches. He went Best of Winners from Senior Puppy the day following the National (under Mrs. Thelma Brown), and was the supported entry for the Texas Staffordshire Club. He also won the Puppy class at the National and at the show which preceded it. His championship was completed in seven more shows in a most auspicious manner, as he took the breed from the classes at five of these shows, in addition to picking up a couple of strong Group placements.

Crunch was then temporarily retired for a growing up period, which came to an abrupt end when John offered Lenna a trip to the Specialty as a birthday gift, if she would like to show Crunch there. She accepted and Crunch brought home the award of Best of Opposite Sex to Best of Breed from Mrs. Annemarie Moore. As he was only 13 months old at the time, Crunch was returned to the mothballs to await full maturity. Lenna comments that Sooner dogs are a bit slow in reaching their potential, but when they do, they seem to hold their excellence forever.

Ch. Byron's Finn McCool taking Best of Breed at Newton K.C. in 1985. Owned by Eva Lydick of Finwar Kennels.

Int. Ch. Herring's Beau Jangles winning Best of Breed over an entry of 41 at the prestigious Montgomery County K.C. Dog Show for All-Terriers in October, 1985; Steve Shaw judging. Beau belongs to the WildWind Kennels, owners, Chester and Lauraine Rodgers, Chepachet, RI.

WILDWIND FARM

WildWind Farm started out in 1974 as Rhody's Amstafs, housed in a fourth floor apartment with three dogs. One of these dogs was a purchase from Sooner Kennels in Oklahoma, at the time when it was still owned by Lois Smith. This dog gained the title to become Champion Sooner's True Grit of Rhody, doing so in five shows of which three were "majors," handled to these wins by his owner, Chet Rodgers. True Grit has, in the Sooner tradition, produced many fine champions over the years including U.C.D. (United Kennel Club C.D.) Champion WildWinds Midnight Revenge, C.D., Champion WildWinds Apache Brava (now living in Hong Kong), Champion Ameretta and Cream, and Champion X-Pert Mogan Romsy. True Grit is now enjoying the life of leisure, living in full retirement at WildWind Farm.

It was during 1983 that numerous changes took place for Chet Rodgers and his dogs, the most important of which was meeting and marrying a woman who fully shares his interest and enthusiasm for Staffs. She is Mrs. Lauraine Rodgers who, at the time she met Chet was especially interested in Dobermans and whose interest in animals even included ownership of a ten-foot python! It was not long before the Staffs had surpassed the Dobermans in this lady's affections; now she is frequently seen in Staffordshire rings, gaining her share of the awards with her husband.

Chet and Lauraine started a new family, changed the name of their new home in Rhode Island to WildWind, and began to breed and show their Staffs extensively. They also run the kennel as a boarding and grooming establishment and are into obedience training. Since their marriage, the Rodgers have finished more than a dozen dogs to titles in both conformation and obedience.

International Champion Herring's Beau Jangles is a source of particular pride to the Rodgers, having attained eight championship titles and being pointed toward two more. An up-and-coming eight-month-old son of this dog, WildWinds Fan Tom of The Oprai, already has 55 of the 100 needed points for United Kennel Club Champion, and is the newest exciting young star at this kennel. It is the Rodgers's goal to produce show quality American Staffordshires and to promote what they feel is probably the greatest, but most misunderstood, of all breeds of the present time. They love their dogs, enjoy them, and are very proud of their "grand ole breed," which they will continue to support most enthusiastically.

Beau Jangles' half sister, Kinders Blue of WildWind, a blue brindle and white bitch with excellent temperament,

Herring's Red Ruby at age one year. Daughter of Ch. Patton's Red Rock Skillet ex Ch. Patton's Red Bridget, this gorgeous bitch was bred by Robby and Jean Herring and belongs to Chet and Lauraine Rodgers.

finished her AKC championship in just ten days and is now working on acquisition of her United Kennel Club titles, which she is close to attaining.

It is interesting to note that the Rodgers are showing their dogs under both United Kennel Club regulations and those of the American Kennel Club.

STAFFORDSHIRE BULL TERRIERS IN THE U.S.A.

BARKER'S

Barker's Staffordshire Bull Terriers are owned by Linda Barker of Burbank, California.

Ch. Barker's Silverlake Lil, by Ch. Piltdown Bill of Truestaff ex. Ch. Val Verde Cockney Cracker. No. 3 Staff Bull Terrier, 1984. Bred and owned by Linda Barker of Burbank, CA.

Among the distinguished Staffords to be found in this kennel and its history is the well-known bitch, Champion Val Verde Cockney Cracker, who is a daughter of Champion Silverlake Iago from Val Verde Ababa. No. 3 Staffordshire Bull Terrier Bitch for 1984, Cracker is the dam of, among others, Champion Barker's Silverlake Lil, sired by Champion Piltdown Bill of Truestaff; and Champion Barker's Big City Slicker, sired by Champion Piltdown Bill of Truestaff. She was bred by Kay A. Benoit.

Champion Barker's Silverlake Lil was No. 3 Staffordshire, SBTCI 1984. Champion Barker's Big City Slicker, for 1984, was No. 2 Staffordshire Bull Terrier, *Canine Chronicle* System; No. 3 Staffordshire Bull Terrier, Routledge System; and No. 4 SBTCI System.

Other Staffords at Barker's include Bullseye Abomindog (bred by Zane Smith), by Champion Piltdown Bill of Truestaff ex Champion Rannvan's Pride of Rannoch; and Barker's Tank of Aramis, by Reetun's Rufus The Red ex Champion Barker's Silverlake Lil, who is homebred.

BLUE STEEL

Blue Steel Staffordshire Bull Terriers were started by Dennis J. Flynn, now of Dallas, Texas, in 1976 when he was living in San Francisco. It was then that he purchased American and Canadian Champion Mother Lode Gypsophila as a pup from

Mr. and Mrs. Lynn Shalley, Auburn, California. He showed "Piggie" in northern California shows and at a large match in Los Angeles under English judge Dennis Rowland, taking Best Puppy Dog in the 6–9 months class.

Upon moving to Seattle, Dennis Flynn found himself to be one of the two first exhibitors of Staffords in that part of the country. Still later the Flynns moved to Albuquerque and then to Dallas. When the move to Albuquerque was made, Pumptail Excalibur Essie was purchased and became Blue Steel's foundation bitch. She came from the kennels of Tim Michelson, who was then at Fort Defiance and later moved to Illinois.

Mother Lode Gypsophila was the third male Stafford to hold a championship in both the United States and Canada and the first male in the northwest to earn that honor.

Referring back to Essie, her dam was bred in Australia and shipped here in whelp. Her sire, Australian and American Champion Daktari Warchief, C.D.X., won his championship with ease when he was a quite older dog.

The inbred Willie Mark's Miss Orday came from Jim Singleton. Her sire and grandsire, Keystone Beauregard, was bred along lines a lot of the earliest breeders used—a raw-boned, pit-type dog. Thus, Dennis's own breeding has been to create

Blue Steel Alfredo Paiz, "Pete," winning Best of Breed at Fort Worth K.C. in March, 1986, is an example of the type and quality Staff being raised at Blue Steel Kennels of Dennis J. Flynn.

a dog of substance and spark. Blue Steel has now produced pups that have shown well and successfully in the show ring. These include Blue Steel Alfredo Paiz and Blue Steel Aretha (littermates). All of the puppies at this kennel are bred to make excellent pets, companions, and guards. Bloodlines include pure Irish (old family Red) and/or carry the rare blue color and should conform closely to the breed standard.

BUCKLAND

Buckland Staffords, owned by Kriss and Lorraine Richards, Salt Lake City, Utah, is the home of some very nice Staffords.

Residing here are Champion Cresstock Necromancer, C.D., and Lorraine Richards's bitch, Cresstock Our Lady Goldberry, who is a daughter of Champion Reetun's Red Tornado ex

Ch. Cresstock Necromancer, C.D., is a Stafford who works in obedience as well as in the show ring. By Ch. Silverlake Hurricane ex Ch. Cresstock's Delight, he is pictured winning his first "major" from which he completed his title with four majors and four Bests of Breed from the classes. He rated No. 4 Obedience Staff in 1984, the year he complete his C.D. Owner-handler, Kriss M. Richards.

Champion Cresstock's Delight.

"Goldie" is off to a splendid start in the show ring with 14 points (including both majors) at age two years. Her wins include Best of Breed and Best of Opposite Sex awards from the classes.

Necromancer, born in September 1983, is by Silverlake Hurricane ex Champion Cresstock's Delight. He belongs to Kriss Richards and has distinguished himself in obedience as well as in conformation competition. He is working on his C.D.X. In 1984, he was rated No. 4 in obedience under the Delaney System. He, too, was bred by Bonnie Cresse.

Both Lorraine and Kriss Richards are keen enthusiasts of Staffordshire Bull Terriers the world over.

BULLSEYE

Bullseye Kennels, originally at Tempe, Arizona, and now located at Chandler in the same state, are owned by J. Zane Smith who, since the age of 13, has been intensely interested in Staffordshire Bull Terriers. His family had owned a purebred Bulldog for several years which had been purchased by his father from a prominent Bulldog breeder in the Phoenix area.

Initially, Zane was attracted to both the American Staffordshire and the Staffordshire Bull Terriers, thus he did considerable research on the breeds prior to the purchase of his first Stafford.

So it was that in 1975, the year in which the Staffordshire Bull Terrier received full American Kennel Club recognition, Zane acquired from Ed Rowland, Piltdown Kennels in New Jersey, a lovely red bitch. Zane started showing during the second year of AKC breed recognition and eventually made his first bitch a champion, she being Champion Piltdown Miss Equal, by Champion Millgarth Power Pack, C.D., ex Champion Piltdown Red Contessa.

In 1977, Zane came upon good fortune in the form of the purchase of English Champion Reetuns Lord Jim, bred and, at the time of importation, owned by Albert Wood of Reetuns Staffordshires in England. Between 1972 (in England) and 1981 (after four years in America), Lord Jim has accomplished the following: Top Staffordshire Bull Terrier in England, 1974; Top Staffordshire Bull Terrier in America, 1978 and 1979; 7 Bests in Show in England; 9 Challenge Certificates and 7 Reserves, England, 1974 (including Crufts); 157 Bests of Breed; English, American, Canadian, and Mexican Championships; and No. 3 Staffordshire in Canada, accomplished in only 10 shows, 1979. In America, Lord Jim holds multiple Group wins and placements, first Best in Terrier Group win by a Stafford in United States history; and Top Stafford Stud Dog in the United States, 1980. In addition, he is the sire of many Group winners and placers, making him an outstanding Stafford Bull Terrier stud dog in America.

The great Ch. Reetun's Lord Jim, first SBT ever to have won First Place in a Terrier Group in the US, gaining one of his many Bests of Breed with owner-handler, J. Zane Smith.

Captivating the audience and then taking the show, SBTs prove truly the dog of the ring.

Left to right: Rev. Father Harold Kampfer with Ch. Piltdown Keltic Druid receiving the Best of Breed award from judge Anne Rogers Clark. Jeanne Pierrette Dross is shown with future champion Normandie Lady of Shors, receiving Best of Opposite Sex for her first 3-point "major" at only 8 months old. Both Staffs owned by Mrs. Dross.

During the years since its beginning, Bullseye Kennels have also owned more Terrier Group winners than any other kennel in the country, including Lord Jim, Champion Bullseye Red Renegade, and Champion Bullwatch Midnight Geisha.

Other important winners at Bullseye are Champion Bullseye Double Rank (a Group placer and multiple Best of Breed winner); Champion Bullseye Forget-Me-Not; Champion Piltdown Miss Equal; Champion Piltdown Mata Hari (No. 1 Stafford Bull Terrier Bitch in the United States for 1982); Champion Reetuns Iron Duke (English import); Champion Reetuns Iron Maiden (English import); Champion Rannvan's Pride of Rannoch (English import and multiple Best of Breed winner);

The first SBT Winning Brace. Ch. Reetun's Iron Maiden and Ch. Bullseye Forget-Me-Not, owner-handled by J. Zane Smith, Bullseye Kennels of Chandler, AZ.

and Piltdown St. Eve, dam of the Top-Winning East Coast dog, Champion Piltdown Keltic Druid.

Champion Reetun's Iron Magic and Champion Bullseye Forget-Me-Not comprised the first Group-Winning brace in the United States, another honor in which Zane takes pride. Also he notes that the English import, Reetuns Rufus The Red, is a multiple Group-placing Best of Breed winner, was No. 3 Staffordshire Bull Terrier in the United States for 1985 at only one year of age, and was in contention for No. 2 in 1986. In 1986, at the age of 22, Zane received his provisional judging approval for Staffordshire Bull Terriers, making him the youngest Stafford Judge in North America and one of the youngest judges of any breed in the United States. He is one of only three Staffordshire Bull Terrier breeder-judges in the United States, the other two being Dr. John Martin and Judi Daniels.

Champion Reetuns Red Tornado, another successful Stafford to have been imported (in 1977) by Zane, was later sold to Margaret Crowe of Barzak Kennels, Sacramento, California. Tornado, in addition to his own wins, is siring numerous champions.

Through the years, Zane has tried to do "family breeding" from the following dogs: Champion Millgarth Power Pack, the English import who is the foundation stud for all

Ch. Davenhill's Adamant Angus, by Ch. Starzend Zodiac Force ex Ch. Guardstock's Witches Double, completed his AKC title at age one-and-a-half years. Little brother to Ch. Davenhill's Firebrewed Rowdy. Owner, Daryl L. Davenport of Sun Valley, CA.

Piltdown breeding; English Champion Bandit's Brintiga (1960s); English Champion Eastaff Danom (1960s); and—very important—Elvinor Miranda, the foundation bitch of Albert Wood's Reetuns Staffords in England. Miranda is the dam of English, American, Canadian, and Mexican Champion Reetuns Lord Jim, English Champion Reetuns Aristocrat, English Champion Reetuns Buffalo Bill (brother to Lord Jim and exported to Italy), Champion Reetuns Iron Duke (English import), Champion Reetuns Iron Maiden, and Champion Reetuns Red Tornado. Tornado sired eight American champions including Champion Bullseye Double Rank; Champion Kalliopes El Torito

Rojo, and Champion Starzend Zodiac Force. Miranda is double granddam of Reetuns Rufus The Red.

DAVENHILL

Davenhill Kennels were established in 1969 as a boarding, grooming, and breeding kennel specializing in Staffordshire Bull Terriers and Cardigan Welsh Corgis. The owners are Daryl L. "Jim" Davenport and Robert W. Phillips, the kennel location is Sun Valley, California.

The first Staffords here were two who became famous among the trailblazers for the breed—Champion Silverlake Gemstock and Champion Silverzend Satan. Both Gemstock and Satan completed their championships during 1975, the

Ch. Kingsblood Royal Val, by Smytan Striker ex Leoline Little Lady, bred by Jerri Marsh. The foundation bitch of Dr. Martin's Doc's Winners, she places Group Fourth under judge Florise Hogan. To the Martin's knowledge, Val was the first Staff bitch to place in the Terrier Group.

first year in which Staffordshire Bull Terriers competed under their own classification at American Kennel Club Dog Shows. Both of these splendid Staffords were sired by Bringarry Dangerman, Gemstock being from Priffdinas Petrina while Satan's dam was Champion Constable's Billy Club of Silverlake.

Also among the Staffordshire Bull Terriers being used successfully in the Davenhill breeding program are: Champion Guardstock's Witches Double and Champion Guardstock's Samson Kenmore (the half brother and half sister of the notable Best in Show winner Champion Guardstock's Red Atom), Champion Logan's Jack Thrasher, Champion Davenhill's Firebrewed Brody and litter brother Champion Davenhill's Adamant Angus, Champion Davenhill's Rikki Tikki, and Champion

Davenhill's Silverlake Lisa.

Champion Silverzend Satan holds a position of special prominence in the history of Staffordshire Bull Terrier development in the United States. A champion in 1975, Satan became Top Dog among Staffordshire Bull Terriers for 1975, 1976, and 1977; Top American-bred 1975-1978; and Top Staffordshire Bull Terrier Stud Dog for 1979. His list of champion progeny is an impressive one, not only in numbers, but in quality and future influence on the breed as well. It includes: Champion Starzend Moondust, Champion Peck's Toshia Luckey, Champion Logan's Jack Thrasher, Champion Starzend Wonder Witch, Champion Logan's Molly Thrasher, Champion Agincourt Annie Oakley, Champion Trugrip Cotton Futures, Champion Starzend Martian Master, Champion Davenhill Silverlake Lisa, Champion Starzend Waltzing Matilda, Champion Davenhill Silverlake Dawn, Champion Starzend Satan's Mistress, Champion Logan's Cock O'The Walk, Champion Davenhill Silverlake Raven, and Champion Peck's Pimpernel of Stonefort.

Davenhill dogs have been used in numerous television appearances for both commercial advertising and series programs, as well as in motion pictures. In September, 1982, Davenhill was featured on the NBC network national show, *Fight Back*, with David

Horowitz. The show pictured Davenhill as an ideal kennel for dog-related services as compared to the typical puppy mills.

DOC'S

Doc's Staffordshire Bull Terriers are owned by John H. Martin, D.V.M., and are located at Kokomo, Indiana. The foundation bitch for this kennel is still with the Martins at age twelve years. She is Champion Kinsblood Royal Val, a daughter of Symtan Striker ex Leoline Little Lady, who was bred by Jerri Marsh and whelped on Christmas Eve in 1973. Val has proved an invaluable member of the Martin family as a companion, a show bitch, and a producer of champions.

To the best of Dr. Martin's knowledge, Val was the first bitch of her breed in the United States to place in a Terrier Group. She did so under Florise Hogan on March 21, 1976.

The first litter of the Martins was from Val by Champion Filmore Tuffy. There were five puppies in the litter, born in June, 1976. Champion Doc's Little Butch was among them, as was Doc's Little Irma (the only bitch) and an excellent male with 14 points when his owners decided to discontinue showing him.

Champion Doc's Little Irate Irene is the result of Val's having been bred to her son, Butch. She was born on February 2, 1977, and became a champion at the very early age of ten months and two days, at that time the youngest champion in the breed. She enjoyed a winning career which included numerous Terrier Group placements.

A litter brother of Irene's, Champion Doc's Little Grundoon, sired a well-known winner in Champion Lochness Ravoon Buster, whose dam was Champion Davenhills Silverlake Raven (a double granddaughter of the nice English import, Bringarry

Ch. Doc's Little Butch, by Ch. Filmore's Tuffy ex Ch. Kingsblood's Royal Val was from the first litter of Staffs born at Dr. John H. Martin's kennel (June 21, 1975). He is owned by the Langlois and lives in Louisiana.

Dangerman). Buster and his notable littermate, Champion Lochness Ravoona Lady, were bred by Tom and Shelley Lochner.

Champion Doc's Little Fancy Lynn (Champion Milgrath Power Pack, C.D.- Champion Kingsblood Royal Val) is the dam of Masebo's Awesome Alice, who completed her championship as the

Staffordshire Bull Terrier Club supported entry at Logansport in 1984. Alice's sire, Champion Lochness Ravoon Buster was Best of Breed; Alice was Winners Bitch, Best of Winners, and Best of Opposite Sex, under judge Mrs. Judi Daniels.

Dr. Martin is a highly respected authority on Staffordshires, and a well-liked judge.

DRAGONQUEST-NAZAN

Dragonquest and Nazan Kennels, which joined forces as breeders of Staffordshire Bull Terriers in the early 1980s, intensely linebreeds Rapparee bloodlines to produce a balanced dog that can move well. Cindy Crawford, Apple Valley, California, is the owner of Dragonquest; Nazan is owned by Nancy Lee.

The kennel's original Staffordshire Bull Terriers were purchased from Mrs. Barbara Elder who owns the great Champion Silverlake Gypsy Queen and were sired by the English import, Truestaff Orchid Challenger, who tragically died before his impact on the breed in America could really be felt.

Champion Ka Nakht Jack O'Diamonds, the young dog who was originally purchased for Dragonquest by Cindy Crawford, is now the center of all the many accomplishments of Dragonquest and Nazan. He is Cindy's first champion and went on to become Top Staffordshire Bull Terrier in the

United States for 1982. He is to be found behind all but four of the Staffs at Dragonquest-Nazan. Jack O'Diamonds is a son of Orchid Challenger ex Gypsy Queen.

Jackie's young son, Nazan's Double Dynamo, seems to be following in his sire's pawprints, both in quality and in his love of dog shows. On his third time in the ring, he went Best of Breed over an excellent entry at Pasadena on June 1, 1986. He is a product of inbreeding between Champion Ka Nakht Jack O'Diamonds and Ka Nakht Moss Rose. (Moss Rose has gained both "majors" and has earned several Best of Opposite Sex wins over "specials.") "Dynamo" himself has also been going strong at the shows with Best of Breed over "specials" from the classes on several occasions. He and his mother are a spectacular pair.

Cindy and Nancy are enthusiastic fanciers who have some splendid stock with which to work.

NORMANDIE

Normandie Staffordshire Bull Terriers at Albany, New York, are owned by Mrs. Jeanne Pierrette Dross who did much to popularize the breed in the New York and New England areas. This kennel is the home of the famous Champion Piltdown Keltic Druid, who was born on February 12, 1978. He was purchased by Mrs. Dross from his breeders, the Edward

BEST OF
BREED

PASADENA
KENNEL CLUB
JUNE 1986

MISSY PHOTO

Nazan's Double Dynamo, en route to his title winning Best of Breed over "Specials" at Pasadena, June, 1986, from the Bred-by-Exhibitor Class. By Ch. Ka Nakht Jack O'Diamonds ex Ka Nakht Moss Rose. Bred and owned by Nancy Lee, Nazan's Staffs.

Rowlands of Piltdown fame.

"Patton," as the little dog is known, is a son of English, American and Canadian Champion Reetun's Lord Jim ex Piltdown St. Eve. Making his ring debut when only six months old at the prestigious Staffordshire Bull Terrier Club of Northern New Jersey Specialty Match in August, 1978, he created considerable stir and much admiration when he won Best Puppy in Sweepstakes under Frank Green, then Best Puppy in Match under Mrs. Judi Daniels.

In autumn 1978, Patton hit the point shows, completing his title at age 15 months. During 1979, he was ranked No. 7 Staffordshire Bull Terrier Dog in the United States and he was No. 2 in East Coast competition despite his extreme youth. In 1980, he was ranked No. 3 Dog among Staffordshire Bull Terriers in the United States and moved up to Top Staffordshire Bull Terrier Dog in eastern competition (Staffordshire Bull Terrier Club point system figured on number of Staffords defeated in breed competition). In 1981, Mrs. Dross retired Patton from competition in order to start out his daughter, Normandie Ides of March. Plus, she

GROUP FIRST

MOBERLY MO.
KENNEL CLUB
1986
PHOTO BY PETRULIS

MOBERLY MO. KC

TERRIER

First in the Terrier Group at Moberly, MO, in October, 1986, was another victory for Ch. Anthenian Angel, a top all-time winning SBT in the US. This English-bred multi-Group winner is by Eng. Ch. Peg's Boltun Trip (Top Staff in England for 1982) ex Kenwun Supreme, thus she is a double-granddaughter of Eng. Ch. Hurricane of Judael, Top Staff in England, 1976. Marcia Foy awards owner-handler Joe LeBlanc.

wanted to withdraw Patton from the shows while at his peak so that he would be remembered by judges and his other admirers that way.

Ides, bred by Mrs. Dross, was by Patton from Champion Normandie Lady of Shars, daughter of Champion Bullseye Red Renegade ex Kalliope's Autumn Nocturne. She finished her title in good order, gaining her first points as a seven-month-old puppy.

To her owner's knowledge, Champion Normandie Lady of Shars was the youngest Staffordshire Bull Terrier in the United States to have completed title when she did, having gained her final points, after two months showing, at age nine months.

SANS TACHE

Sans Tache Staffordshire Bull Terriers at Rockford, Illinois, are owned by Joe and Cheryl LeBlanc.

Although Joe had been involved in various breeds, it was not until 1979 that he was introduced to the Staffordshire Bull Terrier, and not until mid 1980 that he became involved in the dog show ring.

By one system or another, Joe LeBlanc has been associated with the No. 1 Stafford since 1980. Additionally, he has either bred, imported, or owned the stud behind many of the top-ranking Staffords in the United States. This includes the famed **Best in Show-winning Champion Guardstock's Red**

Atom and Champion Athenian Angel, these two being outstanding as among the Top Dog and Top Bitch Staffordshire Bull Terriers in the United States show rings.

During 1984, Champion Diamond's Hot Wax of Sans Tache was the No. 1 Staffordshire Bull Terrier Bitch in America.

As a youth in western Connecticut, Joe hunted with his German Shorthaired Pointers, Labradors, and Beagles. Other breeds owned by him previous to the Staffords included the Pit Bull Terrier and a variety of loving mutts and various mixtures.

Champion Athenian Angel, imported from Yorkshire, represents breeding hand-picked by Joe LeBlanc to complement the Sans Tache breeding program. She, at only two years of age, was a multiple Group placer and Group winner and Top Bitch in 1985 breed and group systems.

Joe LeBlanc is a fancier who firmly believes in *not* being content to live on one's laurels, and that one must prove oneself by constantly winning with new, hopefully even better, dogs each generation. His feeling that "you are only as good as your last victory" is certainly the proper one for success, and it is working out well for Joe.

The foundation stock at Sans Tache is strongly based on George Earle's Judael strain, Jean Short's Craighollows, Marion Forester's Loggerheads

(New Zealand stock), and the Wystaffs owned by Dorene Calhoun and Gwen Gallimore. Bill Morely and Eb Pringle and other winning kennels have played their role in Sans Tache's success by giving advice and sending choice dogs and bitches to Joe for his breeding program.

Eng. Ch. Allendale King, owned by Joe LeBlanc, was the Top Staff in England, 1984.

It is a source of pleasure to Joe LeBlanc that Staffordshire Bull Terriers are becoming so well established in Terrier Groups competing with other breeds. Staffords have a dedicated, devoted friend in Joe whose enthusiasm and energy are certain to produce quality Staffords for many years to come.

BEST IN SHOW

Ch. Guardstock's Red Atom has just won the historic first American Best in Show for a member of the breed; Red Atom is pictured in the arms of Bill Daniels alongside the Best in Show judge, Ann Stevenson. Co-owners Joe LeBlanc and Judi Daniels, handler.

STARZEND

Starzend, the only AKC-registered kennel prefix for Staffordshire Bull Terriers, is the highly successful kennel owned by Judi and Bill Daniels at Arleta, California.

It is from here that the first AKC champion of this breed was owned and shown. That memorable bitch, Champion Northwark Becky Sharp, was imported from Australia. A daughter of West Riding Alfalfa ex Champion Loggerhead's Filanda (representing Marion Forester's illustrious kennel in New Zealand), she served her breed well and produced eight American champions for the Daniels.

Over the years, Starzend has been the home of more than 30 champions, including 22 homebred champions. Among the early ones were Mexican and American Champion Starzend Faultless; Starzend King's Crystal, who gained C.D.X. degrees in obedience; Champion Starzend Deacon; Champion Starzend Headliner; Champion Starzend Isadora; and Champion Starzend Fred Again. (The last four gained their honors in 1976.) Champions Starzend Ivan The Red and Midnight Gertie finished the following year. In 1978, it was Waltzing Matilda, Kaptain Kirk, Jimdandy, and Moondust who kept the new champions banner for Starzend flying high. Champion Bulwatch So Good of Starzend finished in 1979, while the 1980s started with Champion Starzend Satan's Mistress. Champion Starzend Taurus came to the front in 1981. Champion Guardstock's Red Atom completed title that same year.

Various other Starzend dogs have finished for the Daniels since that time, but during the past five years Red Atom has been star of the show as he has amassed an impressive record for the Daniels and for Joe LeBlanc, his co-owner.

Red Atom was born March 20, 1980, by Darton of Henstaff ex Wystaff Witchcraft. He was bred by Ed Strand and gained his title under the ownership of Joe and Cheryl LeBlanc. The co-

Ch. Guardstock's Red Atom, a credit to both Judi Daniels and Joe LeBlanc. Photo by Missy Yuhl.

ownership of this dog by Judi Daniels and Joe LeBlanc has proven exciting beyond words. Atom has gained a total, now, of 133 Group placements, 25 times *first* in the Terrier Group, and, as frosting on the cake, has become the first Staffordshire Bull Terrier to win Best in Show at an AKC championship event. He has been widely acclaimed for his conformation, quality, and temperament, as well as for his physical characteristics and ring presence.

STEINSTAFF

Steinstaff Staffordshire Bull Terriers are in Michigan City, Indiana, where they are owned by Ellis and Faith Steinman. Actually, the kennel consists of only two Staffords, but they are very special ones whose accomplishments in the obedience and dog show worlds are most impressive.

Champion Pumptail Dragonstar Dancer, U.D., Canadian C.D.X., was born on April 7, 1980, by Strathstar Aggressor ex American and

Ch. Pumptail Dragonstar Dancer, U.D., Can. C.D., receiving the Award of Distinction for three consecutive scores of 195 or better on September 1, 2, and 3, 1984. Owned by Ellis and Faith Steinman, trained and handled by Faith.

Australian Champion Pumptail Stardancer. She was imported "in dam" from Australia, born in the United States, and is officially an Australian-bred.

Dancer was originally purchased by Mr. and Mrs. Steinman as a companion for their three children and was enrolled in a basic obedience class to learn control. Previous to owning Dancer, the Steinmans had owned an American Pit Bull registered with the United Kennel Club. (They had wanted a short-coated house dog and had not realized that breeding and temperament were so very vital in being able to live with the animal, no matter what the breed may be.) Getting involved personally with the training of her Staffordshire

was far more rewarding and beneficial, Faith Steinman found, than sending a dog to be trained by someone else, as she had done with the Pit Bull.

At the age of ten months, Dancer began her training at the Trail Creek Dog Training Club in Michigan City, Indiana. This was in February of 1981. After the first ten-week training session, the instructors recognized Dancer's potential and encouraged Mrs. Steinman to take an advanced session. After Dancer's training, the Steinmans were again encouraged to go further, in this case to enter their first Sanctioned Match, where they received a trophy, ribbons for first place, and a score of 190½ in the Novice A Class. Faith Steinman was hooked! She and

Faith Steinman was unable to show her two Staffs herself at Northeastern, IN, in May, 1984, so two friends took them there for her. The results? Future Ch. Steinstaff Goin' For The Gusto (eight months old) went from the Puppy Class to Best of Winners, while kennelmate Ch. Pumptail Dragonstar Dancer, U.D., was Best of Opposite Sex to Best of Breed.

The mighty Ch. Reetun's Lord Jim made exciting records for his breed during his show career in England, Canada, Mexico and the United States. Owned and usually handled by J. Zane Smith, Bullseye Kennels.

Dancer did fun matches for awhile, then entered their first AKC Trial on June 14, 1981. Six months after starting obedience training Dancer acquired her C.D. with scores of 193½ (third place), 194½ (second place), and 195½ (third place) on November 7, 1981.

Now the real challenge began—teaching Dancer to retrieve on command. Oh, it was fun alright to chase her ball and bring it back to be thrown again, but it was another story when it came to retrieving a dumbbell. The day finally came when Faith thought that Dancer was ready for the big time. They entered their first Open A trial, but the balloon soon burst when Dancer did not drop on the recall. That was corrected, but then the next two times Dancer entered she did not qualify as she would not sit for the required three minutes. After working on

these minor problems, Dancer finally got her act together and qualified at the next three shows for her C.D.X. Her first leg was earned on May 15, 1982, and her degree completed on May 30, 1982.

Meanwhile, Dancer earned a three-point major toward her conformation championship. Knowing that the training in Utility would take time, Mrs. Steinman decided to work for the conformation title first, which Dancer completed with her second major on March 27, 1983.

During her show career, Dancer acquired a very satisfactory number of Bests of Breed over strong competition from the males. She received her first Group placement under Phil Marsh.

In April 1983, the Utility competition was tackled. After an early failure, that degree, too, was quickly earned. Then

Dancer earned her Canadian C.D.X.

Dancer was the No. 1 Obedience Staffordshire in America for 1981. She was the first of her breed to gain both a conformation championship and a Utility degree.

American and Canadian Champion Staffordshire Goin' For The Gusto is Dancer's son, sired by the notable Best in Show winner, Champion Guardstock Red Atom. At age six months, he made his show debut by going Best of Breed over a special in Louisville, Kentucky, then finished his championship from the Puppy Class at the age of 11 months. The next day, his owner's birthday, he took his first Terrier Group placement. By the end of 1984, he had accumulated five Group placements including a First in Group.

In 1985, he picked up the challenge of obedience and was successful. He now is a conformation champion in both the United States and Canada and holds C.D.'s from both countries.

By the end of 1985, Gusto had amassed a total of 19 Group placements in the United States, plus three Group

S'N'S Firehawk, by Ch. S'N'S Ogre Easy ex Ch. Rogadame's Third Addition. This bitch was bred by Ron Salle; owned by Jack Robinson and Lenna S. Hanna, Tulsa, OK. Handled here by Jack to Winners Bitch and Best of Opposite Sex at her first point show. Also Jack's first show! Pictured at 13 months, Firehawk is from Easy's first litter.

placements in Canada. By June, 1986, at age 2½, his total stood at 25 Group placements.

WIN-R

WIN-R Staffordshire Bull Terriers are owned by Judy Keller at Fort Collins, Colorado. They are based on dogs of Barzak breeding.

Judy's first two Staffords both became Champion-C.D. winners. Champion Barzak's Wild Reginald, C.D., and Champion Barzak's Lady Winifred, C.D., are half brother and half sister, both bred by Ann Adam. Ann is Judy's sister and a good friend of Barry Crowe, founder of Barzak Staffords.

To date, Judy has bred only one litter, and the first born of that litter looks to be a real winner. He is WIN-R's I'm a King Bee and is by Champion Guardstock's Red Atom from Judy's Champion Barzak's Lady Winifred, C.D.

WIN-R's I'm a King Bee finished his championship at 17 months of age, with all points

En route to his title, Ch. WIN-R I'm A King Bee showing off his type and balance as he takes Best of Winners at Terre Haute in 1985. Judy Keller, owner.

GROUP FIRST
OKLAHOMA CITY
KENNEL CLUB
1986
PHOTO BY PETRULIS

OKLAHOMA CITY KC
TERRIER

Ch. Bar-Gray's Lucifer Sun, by Mount Shire Butcher Block ex Mount Shire Foxy Farrah, an Am Staff bred by James T. Meredith, is pictured with his handler, Dick McKenney, winning First in the Terrier Group at Oklahoma City K.C. in 1986. Owned by Abigail T. Blackwell, Dr. Yvonne Pine, and C. Curts.

won from the Bred-by-Exhibitor Class, including two major wins at age ten months at Staffordshire Bull Terrier Club-supported entry events. He gained his first Terrier Group placement from the Bred-by-Exhibitor Class and won two more Group placements by age 19 months. The future looks bright for this splendid young dog!

VAL VERDE

Val Verde Staffordshire Bull Terriers, Woodinville, Washington, are owned by Kay A. Benoit, whose first litter of the breed was born in 1976.

Kay purchased Champion Shadoplay Dark Destiny, by Champion Silverlake Diablo ex Shortblok Zoril, in January 1974 as a puppy. At that time, she had owned many different dogs of many different breeds, but only as pets. When she bought "Desty" she did so because she wanted a dog that would travel with her and be a protection dog, with a temperament that would not be aggressive to children. She had several friends with small children who visited her frequently, and she did not want a dog around who would harm anyone.

When Kay brought Desty

home, a friend of hers took one look at the puppy and said, "You paid money for that? You could have gone to the pound and gotten something like it." Kay did not agree. Of course, the breed had just been accepted by the American Kennel Club, and it was not, at that point, well known.

Kay's plan had been that after about six months she would have Desty spayed, since she entertained no thoughts of showing or breeding. One day, the same friend who had been so uncomplimentary to Desty in the beginning brought to Kay's a book containing the breed standard. Making careful comparison between the dog and the standard, she said Desty appeared to be good, and maybe Kay should check with someone before spaying. They went to their first puppy match and spoke with Judi Daniels, who had worked so hard to get recognition for the breed. Judi agreed that Desty should be shown and that Champion Tinkinswood Imperial (Desty's grandsire on one side and great grandsire on the other) would be a good choice for stud. To finish up the day, Desty won Best Junior Puppy in Match.

Desty's first litter produced Val Verde Ababa, who was, in due time, bred to her half brother, Iago, also by Imperial but whose dam was Northwark Silverlake. That litter produced Champion Val Verde Cockney Cracker.

Next, Ababa was outcrossed to linebred Champion Barzak's Wild Jim which produced Val Verde Dapper Diplomat. Cockney Cracker, bred to another dog of Barzak breeding, Champion Bobo's Gallant Gladiator, produced a bitch, Val Verde Eureka.

Eureka, bred to Dapper Diplomat, produced what Kay

Tracy Dineley and Ch. Coalminer's Mystery Man, by Topcroft Minstrel ex Ch. Peck's Sexy Pants, bred by Evelyn Frei of Coalminer Kennels. Tracy lives in Aurora, Ontario, Canada.

Ch. Val Verde
Hesione and
Val Verde
Gentry, two
handsome
SBTs, owned
by Kay A.
Benoit.

Benoit had been working for since the beginning: dogs with a more typey head and a more pronounced stop, with good bone structure. From this litter came Val Verde Gentry and Val Verde Gidgit.

Champion Val Verde Hesione was sired by Champion Trugrip Saxon (Champion Silverlake Iago-Trugrip Seattle Sue) and her dam was Val Verde Eureka. The litter sister of Champion Val Verde Hesione is Champion Trugrip Hagar of Val Verde.

Thus, Kay Benoit has spent years working for the improvement of her Staffordshire Bull Terriers. She breeds usually one litter a year from her stock. Although she controls the choice of sire and dam of these litters and is the breeder, all litters are not born in her own household. Kay takes great pride in having succeeded at producing the type of Staffs she wants while maintaining their excellent temperament.

Aust. Ch. Deadgame Ned Kelly working out. A third generation winner of the Sydney Royal Easter Show; a multiple in Group and in Show winner, already noted as a sire of excellence. Deadgame Staffs, of New South Wales, Australia.

The Breeds in Australia and New Zealand

Australia and New Zealand each have a very active and successful nucleus of interest in Staffordshire Bull Terriers. We also understand that American Staffordshire Terriers have recently appeared in Australia, where we hope that the breed will be equally successful.

We have several Australian kennel stories for you which will bring you up to date on what is taking place in Stafford circles there. The number of top American breeders who owe some of their leading winners to Staffords from "down under" is notable. In fact, let us not forget that the first American Kennel Club Champion in the breed, Starzend Becky Sharp, was an import from Australia. Obviously Great Britain provided excellent, quality breeding stock to Australia and New Zealand, and the breeders in those countries used it to their best advantage!

New Zealand Champion Wellwisher of Wystaff, imported from England, brought with him the bloodlines of his respected sire, the multiple champion producer English Champion Rapparee Rothersyke Vow. English Champion Staff McMichael sired the lovely bitch (from Wystaff Worthy), New Zealand Champion Loggerhead's Pensnett, also an influential Stafford of quality. English Champion Buccaneer Shoemaker earned New Zealand and Australian titles in short order. He sired, among others, Australian Champion Gamestar Vagabond, the sire, in turn, of Australian Champion Northwark Joyous. Bred to Australian Champion Almajon Stargazer, Joyous produced American and Australian Champion Pumptail Stardancer, the dam of American Champion Pumptail Dragonstar Dancer, U.D.,

Indeed the first Stafford to gain American championship was an Australian import—Australia received excellent stock from Great Britain and used it to their best advantage.

Top: Ch. Doc's Little Irate Irene taking Best of Breed under English judge Joyce Shorrock. Bred, owned, and handled by Dr. John H. Martin. Twenty-one Staffords assembled for this event; the Martins's four dogs accounted for Best of Breed, Best of Opposite Sex, Winners Dog and Winners Bitch, and Reserve Winners Dog. Mrs. Shorrock bred Eng. Ch. Eastaff Danom, a premier sire in the breed. *Bottom:* Piltdown Mata Hari at one year of age. Winners Bitch at Scottsdale Dog Fanciers Association, owner-handled by J. Zane Smith.

Ch. Guardstock's Samson Kenmore, a fine Stafford owned by Robert M. Randall.

Canadian C.D.X.

Pumptail Staffordshires, which originated in Australia around the mid-1970s, are now located in the United States. Their owner, Timothy F. Michelson of Elgin, Illinois, offers American and Canadian breeders the opportunity to use or acquire stock descended from the top Australian bloodlines. Mr. Michelson's stock includes descendants of Australian Champion Daktari Brutus, through the Brutus grandson, Australian and American Champion Daktari Warchief, an Australian

Deadgame Kingstown at age eight weeks, by Aust. Ch. Deadgame Ned Kelly ex Wilrasyt Deandar Lass. Owned and bred by Deadgame Staffords, New South Wales, Australia.

import, and the New Zealand Champions, Mountainash Xmas Ajax and Mountainash Christmas Aray. Others are Australian Champions Yegans Lad, Loggerheads Jim Crow, Loggerheads Helle, Loggerheads Nekron, Weamera Cyclone, Marabank Diamond Lil, and Gamestar Vagabond.

There could not possibly be a fancier more widely admired and loved than Mrs. Marion Forester, owner of the world famous Loggerhead Kennels in New Zealand. The death of this lady in the mid-1980s was a sad occasion indeed for Stafford fanciers around the world, as the good influence of Loggerhead had been felt worldwide. Mrs. Forester bred, owned, or imported some of the truly key dogs in down under breeding programs. For example, her English importation, Australian and New Zealand Champion Wellwisher of Wystaff, was the sire of every award winner but one (an import) at the Stafford Specialty in New Zealand during 1982. The tradition was carried on at the August 1985 Specialty of the same club with Wellwisher daughters being the dams of practically every award winner at that event.

At the 1985 event, it was Pitshaft Wiseguy who won the dog Challenge Certificate (C.C.) and Best in Show and became the first winner of the Marion Forester Memorial Trophy for Best of Breed.

The award was particularly appropriate as it honored the breeder (Mrs. Forester) of Champion Loggerheads McMichael—Champion Loggerheads Boolarra, who were Pitshaft Wiseguy's parents.

DEADGAME

Deadgame Staffordshire Bull Terriers were founded in 1974 by Alan Gregory, through whose knowledge and natural showmanship the kennel has become noted for the breeding and exhibiting of quality Staffordshire Bull Terriers. Deadgame is located at Chipping Norton, New South Wales. Originally owned by Alan Gregory and Don Mitchell, the kennel recently acquired a third partner, John Allen, a fancier of the breed for many years.

Type at Deadgame originated basically from one dog and two bitches: Champion Loggerheads Penkridge, Champion Crossguns Bravassa and their offspring, Champion Deadgame Du Vienne. It was the sale of this bitch, Du Vienne, that led Don Mitchell to join forces with Alan Gregory.

The foundation dog, Champion Loggerheads Penkridge, had proved himself to be a handful to two previous kennels and was subsequently sold to and transformed by Alan into a noted Australian Champion. He has a first-rate show career and is the only dog to have captured a double Best Exhibit in Show All Breeds in Sydney and Best Exhibit in Show at the New South Wales Staffordshire Bull Terrier Show. As a sire, he has proved popular and has an impressive list of champions to his credit. He was sired by the well-known English dog Champion Staff McMichael, who was also noted both in the show ring and as a sire. His dam, Wystaff Worthy, was mated in England to Staff

Deadgame Dynasty, by Aust. Ch. Loggerheads Penkridge ex Aust. Ch. Crossguns Bravassa, is a future star, bred and owned by Deadgame Kennels.

McMichael and imported to New Zealand by Loggerhead Kennels.

Champion Crossroads Bravassa was purchased by Alan Gregory from Crossguns Kennels, a purchase which put Deadgame in good stead for the future as breeders. She was a first-class show bitch and like her dam a Challenge Bitch at the New South Wales Staffordshire Bull Terrier Show and Best of Breed at the Sydney Royal Easter Show in 1980. An excellent brood bitch, she produced a succession of fine quality in Champions Deadgame Double Dealer, Deadgame Du Vienne, Deadgame Crimson Cloud, Deadgame Canned Heat, and Deadgame Nuclear Nell, all of whom were not only successful in attaining championship honors but who went on to produce winners.

Bravassa was by Betchgreen Bargee, an importation from Great Britain who had achieved outstanding success as a stud

73

Aust. Ch. Loggerheads Penkridge, at age 11 years. By Eng. Ch. Staff McMichael ex Wystaff Worthy. Bred by Marion Forester and owned by Deadgame Staffordshires— a most dominant, prolific sire.

dog. Her dam, Champion Crossguns Annie Strong, was also a well-performing show bitch and a prolific producer of champions at Crossguns.

Champion Deadgame Du Vienne was the force that kept Deadgame in touch with the other kennels. She was no doubt an all-around better bitch than her dam and had an exciting show career. She, too, took out a Challenge at the Sydney Royal Easter Show.

The untimely death of Du Vienne put her owners and the line, as Don tells us, "in a state of horror." She took it upon herself to "go to ground" after an Australian marsupial called a wombat, entering its den one day and never returning. She did, however, leave behind a handsome son, Champion Deadgame Ned Kelly, and his

brother, Deadgame Assassin. Eventually their sisters, Deadgame Silk Degree and Deadgame Regae, brought the Deadgame bitch line back into perspective, and there is now in the kennel a very promising young bitch called Deadgame Bossy Boots.

Champion Loggerheads Penkridge was the highest award-winning Staffordshire Bull Terrier in Australia to date, with a Best in Show All Breeds and a Best in Show at a specialty show among his honors. He won both awards with equal ease under both all-around and specialist judges. We have heard him referred to as the best imported dog to have graced the Australian show scene.

Champion Crossguns Bravassa was both a well-known dual winner and the point score-winning Brood Bitch of The Year in her time.

Champion Deadgame Du Vienne was admired for his accomplishments as a winner and for helping to set type at Deadgame.

Champion Deadgame Double Dealer was the first homebred champion at Deadgame and a litter brother to Du Vienne. He was successful in the obedience ring as well as in conformation competition.

Others who have played a role in the success of this kennel include Champion Deadgame Crimson Cloud, Champion Deadgame Canned Heat, and Champion Deadgame Buck Rogers. The

widely admired Champion Deadgame Ned Kelly is a third generation winner at the Sydney Royal Easter Show, a multiple in-Group and in-Show winner, and a sire of note.

EVASTAFF

Evastaff Kennels of Staffordshire Bull Terriers are fairly new to the Australian dog world, having been established in 1984 at Cobar in New South Wales. Mark and Wendy Evans are the owners.

The Evans are originally from Tasmania, an island state of Australia. They moved to the mainland of Australia around 1982 and began establishing themselves in the Staffordshire Bull Terrier breed. Prior to moving, they had not owned a Stafford, thus their stock is based entirely on that purchased in the New South Wales area.

They are in the process of moving back to Tasmania where they plan to remain permanently and feel that they now have sufficient stock to take with them. Staffords are a comparatively new breed in Tasmania so the Evans plan to promote and firmly establish the dogs in that region.

The dogs obtained for Evastaff are of the newest bloodlines to have reached Australia from England. Australian Champion Nitemarch Petite Miss, a black brindle, was born September 22, 1984. She gained her Australian title at age 18 months, showing a lot of

Crossguns Artful Dodger napping with a friend. Staffordshire Bull Terriers can be good friends with other canines under proper supervision. Deadgame Kennels of Australia.

potential in the ring and winning many worthy Group awards. She is in whelp to Australia's newest English import, Rocellio Captain Morgan, owned by Crossguns Kennels at Sydney.

Petite Miss is by Australian Champion Brittany Brass Tacks ex Australian Champion Airdstock Kate Kelly.

Australian Champion Dorffats Shanrick King is another dog who has done extremely well for the Evans in the show ring. He is a black brindle who was bred by Mr. R. Whalley, Scratchline Staffords, and sired by Crossguns Mr. Peggotty ex Kurnpow Pied Piper.

Special pride at Evastaff is taken in Australian Champion Tuskalear Tunza Strife, a brindle male bred by the Boswells. This dog gained Australian championship at the age of 26 months and has multiple in-Group and in-Show

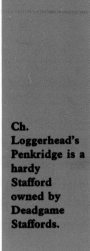

Ch. Loggerhead's Penkridge is a hardy Stafford owned by Deadgame Staffords.

awards. He was Best Intermediate in Show at the Victoria Golden Jubilee Championship Stafford Show in 1985 under an English judge and Reserve Challenge Dog at both the Sydney Easter Royal and the New South Wales Championship Stafford Show in 1986. What top quality placings for a young dog! He is by Australian Champion Wildside Triple Truble ex Australian Champion Brittany Brazen Hussy.

Evastaff Naughty Nell, the latest addition to Evastaff Kennels, was purchased at age six weeks. She is by the English import, Havocson Benjis, from Australian Champion Firestaff No Scruples.

TUSKALEAR

Tuskalear Staffordshire Bull Terriers are owned by G. and M. Boswell at Mortdale, New South Wales. The kennel's first Stafford bitch, Champion Brittany Brazen Hussy, was purchased as a gift for Mrs. Boswell. She had been owned by the Boswells for about a year before they decided to try her out in the show ring where she did quite well and gained her championship.

In due time, Hussy was mated to an Australian Champion, Stafwright Blake, which produced five puppies, including the handsome one who became Australian Champion Tuskalear Broad Boy, a consistent winner of Best of Breed, in-Group, and in-Show.

Brazen Hussy was bred twice following her first litter. Two puppies sired by Australian Champion Wildside Triple Truble and one from an English import, Rocellio Captain Morgan, resulted.

The Boswells have only the one bitch, Hussy, keeping their breeding operations on a small scale.

Champion Tuskalear Broad Boy has been a source of tremendous pride to the Boswells. His victory of Best Exhibit in Show at an all-breed event was a particular thrill, as Mrs. Boswell points out that in Australia not many Staffordshires ever go on to win this top award.

Staffordshire Bull Terriers in Great Britain

The inaugural Specialty show of the Staffordshire Bull Terrier Club took place in England on August 17, 1935. The judge was H. N. Beilby, who found the best of more than 70 entries in Jim the Dandy, owned by Jack Barnard. Jim the Dandy's fame was earned in many ways; his quality led to his becoming the blueprint of the first breed standard. Game Lad, second in the Open Dog Class, was another Staffordshire who had tremendous impact on the breed. Best Bitch at this event was won by Brave Nell; second-place honors went to a bitch named Queenie.

The Staffordshire Bull Terrier Club was founded by some 40 breeders in May, 1935. The organization's early officers were Jack Barnard, president, and Joe Dunn, secretary.

Prior to the first Specialty show, the breed had its own classes at the Hertfordshire Agriculture Society two months earlier, on June 11, 1935. Then, in 1936, came Crufts, which that year included Staffordshires for the very first time. Joe Mallen's Cross Guns Johnson led the field at this event.

Other milestones in early Staffordshire Bull Terrier history included the founding of three additional Specialty clubs: Southern Counties (1937); Northern Counties (1943); and the Northwest Staffordshire Bull Terrier Club in the Manchester area (1946).

The breed's first English Champions gained their titles when the Dog Challenge Certificate was awarded to Champion Gentleman Jim and the Bitch Challenge Certificate was won by Champion Lady Eve. These honors were accomplished at the Birmingham National Show, where Challenge Certificates for the first time were offered for the breed. The winners gained their other two C.C.s for the title at shows almost immediately following Birmingham.

The Staffordshire Bull Terrier Club of Great Britain was founded in May, 1935. Its inaugural Specialty show took place in England on August 17, 1935.

Top: Ch. Cresstock Omega, by Ch. Reetun's Red Tornado ex Ch. Cresstock Delight. Bred by Bonnie Cresse and owned by Debbie Smith. *Center:* Ch. Peck's Sexy Pants, by Peck's Brindled Bandit ex Doomsday Chablis, is handled by Tracy Dineley and owned by Evelyn Frei. *Bottom:* Ch. Pumptail Dragonstar Dancer, U.D., Can. C.D.X., placing under judge Emil Klinckhardt. Owned by Ellis and Faith Steinman. Photo by Booth.

Eng. Ch. Rendorn Drummer Boy of Razemick, a Staffordshire Bull Terrier owned by M. and M. Worthington.

During June, 1946, the first post-World War II championship show for Staffordshires took place, under the auspices of the Southern Counties Staffordshire Bull Terrier Society. Close to a most impressive 300 entries competed. Two months later, the parent club for Staffordshire Bull Terriers held its first championship show, again drawing in close to 300 entries.

Eng. Ch. Ben Hur going Best in Show at the SBT Club Championship Show in 1983. Owner, Mr. R. Austin.

Many outstanding Staffordshire Bull Terriers have been bred and raised in Great Britain since World War II. A number of them, or of their progeny, have come to the United States, where the breed has been immeasurably enhanced by their influence.

MR. AND MRS. R. AUSTIN

Mr. and Mrs. R. Austin are the owners of English Champion Ben Hur, whom they purchased as a puppy for their fourteen-year-old son.

The Austins were introduced to the Northeastern Staffordshire Bull Terrier Club by a friend when Ben was two and one half years old, which started the show career by this grand dog. He quickly earned his title and for further excitement for his owners won two Bests in Show, one at the Staffordshire Bull Terrier Club Specialty Show in an entry of 363 dogs in 1983, the other, two years later in 1985.

Champion Ben Hur is still being campaigned. A puppy by him, Quo Vadis, started out with wins at his first show, the Northeastern Staffordshire Bull Terrier Club Open Show, at age nine months. The pup is also owned by the Austins.

The Austins and their Staffords reside at Fenham Upon Tyne.

MR. T. A. NORTON

Mr. T. A. Norton, Bacup, Lancs, is a great enthusiast of Staffordshire Bull Terriers and owner of some very good ones.

He owns English Champion Topcroft Trailblazer, who gained Best in Show at the Staffordshire Bull Terrier Club (parent club for the breed in England) Golden Jubilee Show. This event was in celebration of the 50th anniversary of the breed's recognition by the Kennel Club of Great Britain and the founding of the Staffordshire Club. This show was a very exciting occasion for all Stafford fanciers and especially for Mr. Norton, as

Eng. Ch.
Topcroft
Trailblazer
went Best in
Show at the
Golden
Jubilee
Specialty.
Owner, T.H.
Norton.

his marvelous bitch won in an entry of 426 Staffordshires. R. W. A. Cairns was the judge of the bitches for the occasion.

Trailblazer is a daughter of Champion Black Tusker, whose record as a sire now stands as having produced the greatest number of champions of the breed in Great Britain. Bred by Harry Latham, Trailblazer is from Solitaire of Topcroft and was born on March 19, 1983. Throughout her show career, Trailblazer was handled in the ring by the Norton's son, Mark, who was thirteen years old when he started showing her and age fifteen when she became a champion.

Among Trailblazer's other important wins are the Bitch C.C. and Best of Breed at Darlington, judge Mrs. J. Shorrocks; Bitch C.C. at Northern Counties, judge Mrs. D. Berry; and several Reserve C.C. awards in keen competition under other noted authorities.

SHEILA AND PETER WALL

Sheila and Peter Wall of Chesterfield, Derby, have been into Staffordshire Bull Terriers since the early 1960s. To quote Peter Wall's own words, "I always tell people to exercise great care when buying birthday gifts for their wives. In 1962, I took the bold step of buying a Stafford puppy for my wife, Sheila, for a present. He went by the name of Peta the Bomber, and he came from Boathouse Kennels in Leicester." Peta was by Wawocan Wundebar out of Topcroft Benita. This made him basically of Champion Major in Command of Wychbury and Champion Goldwyn's Leading Lad breeding. Peta had been purchased as a pet and lived the quiet life until the Walls were offered a mature bitch named Jane's the Girl, whose pedigree sported a vast number of unknown dogs apart from the well-known Champion Chestonian Annoyance and Alan's Dynamo. What Peter and Sheila did not know when they accepted Jane was that she was in season. Peta, however, did notice and proved himself no gentleman. From the resultant litter of five puppies, Peter's brother, Alwyn, took a bitch whom he named Mary Poppins.

It was at this point that the Walls began to take an interest in showing, and consequently, when the time came for Mary Poppins to go into the nursery, Champion Jolihem El Toro was chosen as sire. Alwyn kept a bitch from El Toro—Mary Poppins and named her Queen Bodicea. The choice for a mate for Bodicea was Champion Jolihem Dreadnaught.

Alwyn Wall kept a dog from Dreadnaught—Bodicea, Travwall El Cid, who did a lot of winning without gaining top honors. He then brought in Jolihem Battle Flame who was by Kinderlee Clanaboy ex the Dreadnaught bitch, Jolihem Wicked Lady. Battle Flame's mating to El Cid brought together three main lines and produced the bitch, Travwall Breeders Dream.

Eng. Ch. Goldwyn Leading Star, owned by Peter and Sheila Wall.

J. Zane Smith's Ch. Reetun's Rufus the Red revealing his well-developed chest and confident expression.

Ch. Cresstock Kharisma, by Cresstock Hoss ex Ch. Cresstock Delight, was bred by Bonnie Cresse and is owned by Keri Robison.

Doc's Little Otis, by Ch. Leoline Gallant Hussar ex Ch. Doc's Little Irate Irene, is not in a show home, but could obviously succeed in show competition were he given the opportunity to do so. He is owned by Brian Kline of New Haven, IN.

Next, the Walls had the opportunity to purchase Chapultapec Boy, a puppy by Dennybeck Devil May Care from the hard-bitten bitch Hillstaff Iced Diamond. At the time, the Walls had no room for another Stafford but felt that Chapultapec was too good to leave. He was taken back to Chesterfield and found a home with a Mrs. and Mrs. Chapman. Kept as a pet, he nevertheless fulfilled the promise shown as a puppy, and there was no hesitation in mating Travwall Breeders Dream to him when the time arrived. This mating produced Star Prize, who gave the Walls tremendous pleasure by winning regularly and gaining one reserve Challenge Certificate.

Star Prize was subsequently bred to Champion Red Ru, a decision which gave the Walls the nudge they needed to get them to center stage. A dog and a bitch puppy which looked like what the Walls had been wanting were kept. The Walls' judgment proved correct when the bitch, English Champion Goldwyn Leading Star, gave them a collection of nine Challenge Certificates and, for added excitement, took Best of Breed at Crufts in 1981. Her brother, Goldwyn Golden Lad, who had been given by the Walls to their son Michael in co-ownership with Mr. J. A. Altoft, originator of the Goldwyn line, did less well in the show ring than had been hoped but as a sire surpassed the Walls's highest expectations.

From a mating with Mr. and Mrs. Pugh's bitch, Rocellio Belle Starr, Golden Lad produced Champion Rocellio Miss Supreme, another to gain nine Challenge Certificates. A repeat mating of Golden Lad and Belle Starr produced a daughter who has scored in both the show ring and obedience. She is Canadian Champion Rocellio Miss Scarlett.

Cock 'N' Bull's Poppycock, C.D., half-sister to Blue Monday, was bred by Cock 'N' Bull Kennels, the Browns, Bloomington, CA. Pictured earning an obedience award.

Mr. Cunningham was successful with his bitch, Champion Carstaff Dancing Queen, who was from Sunrise Black Rose. Dancing Queen gained Reserve C.C. at Crufts in 1984, losing out only to the Walls's bitch, Goldwyn Lucky Star, for the Challenge Certificate.

Another English Champion by Golden Lad is Champion Judy of Jolihan, whose dam was Mrs. Tomlinson's Emma of Gal. Mr. and Mrs. Ward have one C.C. with their bitch, Lymstaff Lady Flash of Zabarette, sired by Golden Lad and bred by Mr. and Mrs. Tooby.

The Walls' own Champion Goldwyn Lucky Star, by Champion The Malaser Mauler from Champion Goldwyn Leading Star, has taken four Challenge Certificates, the first of which was gained at Crufts in 1983. She also gained Best of Opposite Sex at the same show. Lucky Star returned the following year to earn the bitch Challenge Certificate and

Above: Rothersyke Jaunty Jake taking the second Group placement won by the SBT breed in the U.S. It was a Group fourth at Farmington, CT in 1975. Bred by Dr. I.W. Davidson of England, "Jaunty" was by Ch. Parraree Look Lively ex Rothersyke Gem. Though one of the finest dogs of his time, he died before attaining his championship. *Opposite:* Ch. Chainman Proteus, by Belnito Ben Hur ex Belnite Beauty, was imported from William. McKnight of Belfast and is owned by Robert Finkel, South Wardsboro, Vermont. Handled by Frank Green.

BEST OF BREED

SOUTHERN ADIRONDACK
DOG CLUB INC

JOE C ≡≡≡≡ AUG 9 1980

forged through to Best of Breed.

The Walls are now considering their future game plan. Due to the potency of Goldwyn Golden Lad, there are many options from which to choose for the future. Peter Wall comments, "It is now 24 years since we began in Staffords, and I sometimes look at my wife and offer up a prayer of thanks. I wonder if she still feels the same after that present of a Stafford puppy all those years ago."

TONDOO

Tondoo Staffordshire Bull Terriers are owned by Mr. Tony Jones at Llanedeyrn, Cardiff, Wales. Included in this kennel is an especially strong team of bitches who have achieved notable successes, both in the show ring and as producers.

English Champion Tondoo Miss Moonshine, born in June, 1983, is a homebred by

Champion Ginnels Black Tuskyana (Champion Black Tusker-Ginnels Maddonnas Moon Maid) ex Ladies and Gentlemen (Bethane Barney Bates-Malstaffs Proud Becky). This lovely bitch was Top Stafford in England during 1985 and is a source of well-justified pride to her breeder-owner.

Miss Moonshine's wins during 1985 include C.C. and Best in Show, South Wales Championship Staffordshire Bull Terrier Club Specialty, judge Mr. Alex Waters; C.C. at Southern Counties Championship Show, judge Mr. Tommy Taylor; C.C. at South Wales K.C. Championship Show, judge Mr. Trevor Rowe; C.C. at Windsor Championship Show, judge Mr. Terry Giles; C.C. Paignton Championship Show, judge Mr. Stephen Rumble; C.C. and Best in Show, Potteries Staffordshire Bull Terrier Club 21st Anniversary Championship Show, judge Mr. Malcolm Boam; and C.C. and Best of Breed, Birmingham Championship Show, judge Mrs. Jean Westwood.

The year 1985 was the Golden Jubilee Year for Staffordshire Bull Terriers in England, adding special excitement to these spectacular wins. In addition, Miss Moonshine broke a record when she gained three of her C.C.s within a period of seven days.

An especially outstanding young bitch for whom Mr.

Ch. Val Verde Cockney Cracker, bred by Kay A. Benoit and owned by Linda B. Barker, Burbank, CA, here is taking points on the way to the title.

VARIETY
GROUP PLACEMENT
MISSISSIPPI COAST
KENNEL CLUB
FALL 1986
PHOTO BY
L. SOSA

MISSISSIPPI COAST

TERRIER

Ch. Bar-Gray's Lucifer Sun, by Mount Shire Butcher Block ex Mount Shire Foxy Farrah, an Am Staff bred by James T. Meredith and owned by Y. Fine, A. Blackwell, and C. Curts. Pictured with handler Dick McKenney, winning a Group placement at Mississippi Coast K.C. 1986, under judge Ron Krohne.

Jones has high hopes is a puppy born during 1986, Tondoo Forget Me Not, by Champion Eastaff Guardian ex Champion Tondoo Miss Moonshine. She may well follow closely in the pawprints of her dam.

Other high quality bitches at this successful kennel include the noted Tondoo War Squaw, Tondoo Hooker, Tondoo Taboo, and Tondoo Guardian Angel.

Staffordshire Bull Terriers in Canada

COALMINER

Coalminer Staffordshire Bull Terriers started their days of winning in Switzerland during 1976. Their owner, Evelyn Frei, and her sister, who is a Staffordshire Bull Terrier breeder in Switzerland, have contributed enormously to quality in the Stafford world.

In Canada, Evelyn Frei's Coalminer dogs are to be found behind some of the most excellent winners. In her start with the breed, Mrs. Frei imported a bitch from Scotland, spending considerable time before making her selection. The bitch she chose was Lanreen Candy May, a red who proved that the two years of Mrs. Frei's searching for "just the right one" were well spent.

After a couple of breedings of Candy May to imported stud dogs, Evelyn Frei decided to purchase an outstanding stud of her own. Thus it was that Topcroft Minstrel, from England's famed Topcroft Kennels, was acquired. He was a very impressive black dog who did well in the show ring as a puppy. Unfortunately, due to an untimely accident, his show career was cut short. Minstrel, however, made his presence strongly felt as a stud dog. Lanreen Candy May was bred to him, which resulted in a gorgeous black.

In 1979, Mrs. Frei, her family and her Staffordshires moved to Canada. Soon after, the first Coalminer blue Staffordshire was born, sired by an English dog. Later, Candy was bred to a black English import by whom she had seven puppies. The smallest bitch was kept and eventually bred to an American dog named Gentleman Jake the Red. From Jake and Candy, Mrs. Frei kept two red bitches who became Champion Coalminer's Red Rose, or "Rosey," and Coalminer's Sadie Lady, or "Sadie." Handled by Tracy

Opposite: Am. and Can. Ch. Steinstaff Goin' For The Gusto, C.D.X., T.D., is an accomplished Staffordshire Bull Terrier owned by Ellis and Faith Steinman.

Ch. Lochness Lonnie McBlue, by Ch. Doc's Little Blue Max ex Ch. Lochness Ravoon Ravoona Lucy, is finishing title here, owner-handled by Patricia A. Farnsworth. Bred by Thomas J. and Shelley Lochner.

Dineley, both made nice records in the Canadian dog show ring.

Candy was bred back to her sire, Topcroft Minstrel, which brought about a stunning litter of reds and blues. From this litter a blue male, "Blueto," was kept, whom Mrs. Frei eventually sent to her sister in Switzerland. Blueto demonstrated early on the makings of an international champion, and competed successfully in Switzerland, England, and Germany.

Next, Mrs. Frei started a search for a bitch who carried the blue gene. She finally purchased Canadian Champion Peck's Sexy Pants, brindle and white pied. At the same time, Mrs. Frei bought an English black and white pied bitch.

"Sexy," bred to Topcroft Minstrel, produced a lovely litter which included a blue brindle that was kept by Mrs.

Frei. The puppy became Champion Coalminer's Blueberry Pie, who finished in four weekends with all Bests of Breed at the age of ten months. Needless to say, the Sexy'— Minstrel breeding was twice repeated, each time with great success. Not only did their litters contain blues—but they were truly *handsome* blues. Two of the puppies from these outstanding litters are Champion Coalminer's Mystery Man ("Meistro") and Champion Coalminer's Boy Minstrel ("Casey"), both of whom are doing well in the ring today. Handled by Tracy Dineley, both dogs finished with Group placements. "Casey," sold to Alex Mudie, finished as a puppy. Meistro was the No. 1 Staffordshire Bull Terrier in Canada for 1986.

Mrs. Frei has now decided to cut back her breeding schedule to a bare minimum and thus

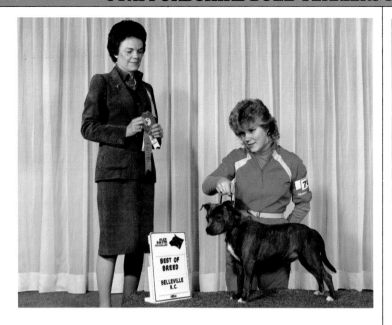

Ch. Coalminer's Blueberry Pie taking Best of Breed at Belleville K.C., in Canada. Ten months old, handled by Tracy Dineley for breeder-owner, Mrs. Evelyn Frei, Coalminer Kennels of Ontario.

has only two dogs. Her handler, Tracy Dineley, finished five Staffordshires and pointed three others in an 18-month period.

With all this "Staffy stuff," as Tracy puts it, coming at her so fast, she could not help but fall in love with the breed. With Evelyn Frei's help, Tracy and her Clandara Kennels will continue the Coalminer line of Staffords that are famous winners all over the world. Tracy is becoming as dedicated to quality as Evelyn Frei is, so in the future look for the new generations of Coalminer-Clandara Staffordshire Bull Terriers.

Aust. and Am. Ch. Daktari War Chief, C.D.X., handled by owner Tim Michelson here is taking Winners Dog and Best of Breed at Rio Grande K.C., 1981.

Staffordshire Terrier Breed Standards

STANDARD FOR THE AMERICAN STAFFORDSHIRE TERRIER

The standard for the Staffordshire Terrier, forerunner to the American Staffordshire Terrier, was approved by the American Kennel Club in June of 1936. Prior to that date, these dogs had been in the United States since the early 1800s, developed from a cross between the old Bull and Terrier and were originally recognized by the United Kennel Club. When recognized by the American Kennel Club, American Staffordshires became the nineteenth Terrier breed.

Following is the standard, effective since 1936, for American Staffordshire Terriers.

General Impression— The American Staffordshire Terrier should give the impression of great strength for his size, a well put-together dog, muscular, but agile and graceful, keenly alive to his surroundings. He should be stocky, not long-legged or racy in outline. His courage is proverbial.

Head— Medium length, deep through, broad skull, very pronounced cheek muscles, distinct stop; and ears are set high.

Ears— Cropped or uncropped, the latter preferred. Uncropped ears should be short and held half rose or prick. Full drop to be penalized.

Eyes— Dark and round, low down in skull and set far apart. No pink eyelids.

Muzzle— Medium length, rounded on upper side to fall away abruptly below eyes. Jaws well defined. Underjaw to be strong and have biting power. Lips close and even, no looseness. Upper teeth to meet tightly outside lower teeth in front. Nose definitely black.

Opposite: Ch. Oltyme's Cock O' The Walk, a famed American Staffordshire Terrier owned by Cock 'N' Bull Kennels.

Neck— Heavy, slightly arched, tapering from shoulders to back of skull. No looseness of skin. Medium length.

Shoulders— Strong and muscular with blades wide and sloping.

Back— Fairly short. Slight sloping from withers to rump with gentle short slope at rump to base of tail. Loins slightly tucked.

Body— Well-sprung ribs, deep in rear. All ribs close together. Forelegs set rather wide apart to permit chest development. Chest deep and broad.

Tail— Short in comparison to size, low set, tapering to a fine point; not curled or held over back. Not docked.

Legs— The front legs should be straight, large or round bones, pastern upright. No resemblance of bend in front. Hindquarters well muscled, let down at hocks, turning neither in nor out. Feet of moderate size, well arched and compact. Gait must be springy but without roll or pace.

Coat— Short, close, stiff to the touch, and glossy.

Color— Any color, solid, parti, or patched is permissible, but all white, more than 80 percent white, black and tan, and liver not to be encouraged.

Size— Height and weight should be in proportion. A height of about 18 to 19 inches at shoulders for the male and 17

Jedediah of Cresstock, by Cresstock Hoss ex Ch. Cresstock Game Lady, was bred by Rebecca Russell and is owned by Lucky and Sharon Durand.

A comparative study in breed conformations: American Staffordshire (*right*) and Staffordshire Bull Terrier (*left*). Owners, Lenna S. Hanna, S'N'S Am. Staffs, and Marion Forrester, Deadgame Staffords.

to 18 inches for the female is to be considered preferable.

Faults— Faults to be penalized are: Dudley nose, light or pink eyes, tail too long or badly carried, undershot or overshot mouths.

STANDARD FOR THE STAFFORDSHIRE BULL TERRIER

The following standard is for Staffordshire Bull Terriers, which breed was admitted to registration by the American Kennel Club in 1974 and whose standard became effective on March 5, 1975, at which time Staffordshire Bull Terriers received their own separate classification at American Kennel Club dog shows.

Characteristics— From the past history of the Staffordshire Bull Terrier, the modern dog draws its character of indomitable courage, high intelligence, and tenacity. This, coupled with its affection for its friends, and children in particular, its off-duty quietness and trustworthy stability, makes it a foremost all-purpose dog.

General Appearance— The Staffordshire Bull Terrier is a smooth-coated dog. It should be of great strength for its size and, although muscular, should be active and agile.

Head and Skull— Short, deep through, broad skull, very pronounced cheek muscles, distinct stop, short foreface,

The noted American Staff, Ch. Steeltown's Blue Monday, who was invited by *Kennel Review* magazine to showcase "the All-American Dog." During his first year as a "Special" out with Mike Shea, his wins included both Group First and Best of Breed at a Specialty. Owned by J.E. and J.A. Brown.

black nose. Pink (Dudley) nose to be considered a serious fault.

Eyes— Dark preferable, but may bear some relation to coat color. Round, of medium size, and set to look straight ahead. Light eyes or pink eye rims to be considered a fault, except that, where the coat surrounding the eye is white, the eye rim may be pink.

Ears— Rose or half-pricked and not large. Full drop or full prick to be considered a serious fault.

Mouth— A bite in which the outer side of the lower incisors touches the inner side of the upper incisors. The lips should be tight and clean. The badly undershot or overshot bite is a serious fault.

Neck— Muscular, rather short, clean in outline and gradually widening toward the shoulders.

Forequarters— Legs straight and well boned, set rather far apart, without looseness at the shoulders and showing no weakness at the pasterns, from which point the feet turn out a little.

Body— The body is close coupled, with a level topline, wide front, deep brisket and well sprung ribs being rather light in the loins.

Hindquarters— The hindquarters should be well

muscled, hocks let down with stifles well bent. Legs should be parallel when viewed from behind.

Feet— The feet should be well padded, strong and of medium size. Dewclaws, if any, on the hind legs are generally removed. Dewclaws on the forelegs may be removed.

Tail— The tail is undocked, of medium length, low set, tapering to a point and carried rather low. It should not curl much and may be likened to an old-fashioned pump handle. A tail that is too long or badly curled is a fault.

Coat— Smooth, short and close to the skin, not to be trimmed or dewhiskered.

Color— Red, fawn, white, black or blue, or any of these colors with white. Any shade of brindle or any shade of brindle with white. Black-and-tan or liver color to be disqualified.

Size— Weight: Dogs, 28 to 38 pounds; bitches, 24 to 34 pounds. Height at shoulders: 14 to 16 inches, these heights

Reetun's Rufus The Red is owned by Bullseye Kennels of J. Zane Smith.

being related to weights. Non-conformity with these limits is a fault.

Disqualifications

Black-and-tan or liver color.

NEW AKC STANDARD, 1990

The first standard for the breed (1975) has been slightly altered to include:

Proportion—In proportion, the length of back, from wither to tailset, is equal to the distance from withers to ground. **Gait**—Free, powerful and agile with economy of effort. Legs moving parallel when viewed from front or rear. Discernible drive from hind legs. This new standard became effective January 1, 1990.

As Staffordshire Bull Terriers originally developed in Great Britain, it is obvious that the American Standard for the breed was based on that which had been accepted for the breed in Great Britain. The following is the first British Standard for the Staffordshire Bull Terrier.

BRITISH STANDARD FOR THE STAFFORDSHIRE BULL TERRIER, 1935

General Appearance— Staffordshire Bull Terrier is a smooth-coated dog, standing about 15 to 18 inches high at the shoulder. He should give the impression of great strength for his size, and, although muscular, should be active and agile.

Owner-handler, J. Zane Smith with Reetun's Rufus The Red placing Best in Group at the Flagstaff K.C. Show. Bullseye Kennels.

Head— Short, deep through, broad skull, very pronounced cheek muscles, distinct stop, short foreface, mouth level.

Ears— Rose, half prick and prick, these three to be preferred, full drop to be penalized.

Eyes— Dark.

Neck— Should be muscular and rather short.

Body— Short back, deep brisket, light in loins with forelegs set rather wide apart to permit chest development.

Front Legs— Straight, feet well padded, to turn out a little and showing no weakness at pasterns.

Hind Legs— Hindquarters well muscled, let down at hocks like a terrier.

Coat— Short, smooth and close to skin.

Tail— The tail should be of medium length tapering to a point and carried rather low; it should not curl much and may be compared with an old-fashioned pump handle.

Weight— Dogs 28 to 38 pounds. Bitches four pounds less.

Color— May be any shade of brindle, black, white, fawn, or red, or any of these colors with white. Black and tan and liver not to be encouraged.

Faults to be Penalized— Dudley nose, light or pink eyes (rims), tail too long or badly curled, badly undershot or overshot mouths.

Scale of Points— General Appearance, coat and condition 15; head 30; neck 10; body 25; legs and feet 15; tail 5; Total 100.

As one who believes very sincerely in the importance of a Scale of Points in helping to place the various breed features in their correct perspective in the minds of breed students, I deplore the disappearance of this scale from the newer British Standard and from the American Standard. I have always felt that such a scale is one of the most important and most easily understandable ways in which a Specialty Club

The noted Ch. Doc's Little Irate Irene, by Ch. Doc's Little Butch ex Ch. Kingsblood Royal Val, who was born February 2, 1977, and is shown here at age ten months, when she completed her title, becoming the youngest Champion of the breed at the time. Owner, John H. Martin.

can point out the importance of one breed characteristic as opposed to another. At the time the first British standard for Staffordshires was written (the mid-1930s), the majority of breed standards used this system, both in Great Britain and in the United States. We feel that the more modern omission of a Scale of Points is a loss and disservice to all of the breeds in which this particular change has occurred. The first British standard for Staffordshire Bull Terriers remained in effect in Great Britain from 1935 until 1949

BRITISH STANDARD FOR THE STAFFORDSHIRE BULL TERRIER

General Appearance— Smooth coated, well balanced, of great strength for his size. Muscular, active and agile.

Characteristics— Traditionally of indomitable courage and tenacity. Highly intelligent and affectionate especially with children.

Temperament— Bold, fearless and totally reliable.

Ch. Bullseye Double Rank taking Best of Breed at Yosemite K.C. in 1982, owner-handled by breeder, J. Zane Smith.

when a new standard for Staffordshire Bull Terriers was approved by The Kennel Club of Great Britain. The new standard obviously has met the needs of the fancy in that it has remained in effect right up to the present time.

Head & Skull— Short, deep through with broad skull. Very pronounced cheek muscles, distinct stop, short foreface, nose black.

Eyes— Dark preferred but may bear some relation to coat

color. Round of medium size, and set to look straight ahead. Eye rims dark.

Ears— Rose or half pricked, not large or heavy. Full, drop or pricked ears highly undesirable.

Mouth— Lips tight and clean. Jaws strong, teeth large, with a perfect, regular and complete scissor bite, i.e., upper teeth closely overlapping the lower teeth and set square to the jaws.

Neck— Muscular, rather short, clean in outline gradually widening towards shoulders.

Forequarters— Legs straight and well boned, set rather wide apart, showing no weakness at the pasterns, from which point feet turn out a little. Shoulders well laid back with no looseness at elbow.

Body— Close coupled, with level topline, wide front, deep brisket, well sprung ribs; muscular and well defined.

Hindquarters— Well muscled, hocks well let down with stifles well bent. Legs parallel when viewed from behind.

Feet— Well padded, strong and of medium size. Nails black in solid-colored dogs.

Tail— Medium length, low set, tapering to a point and carried rather low. Should not curl much and may be likened to an old-fashioned pump handle.

Gait/Movement— Free, powerful and agile with economy of effort. Legs moving parallel when viewed from front or rear. Discernible drive from hindlegs.

Coat— Smooth, short and close.

Color— Red, fawn, white, black or blue, or any one of these colors with white. Any shade of brindle or any shade of brindle with white. Black and tan or liver color highly undesirable.

Size— Weight: Dogs 28 lbs to 38 lbs. Bitches 24 lbs to 34 lbs. Desirable height (at withers) 14 to 16 inches, these heights being related to the weights.

Faults— Any departure from the foregoing points should be considered a fault and the seriousness with which the fault should be regarded should be in exact proportion to its degree.

Note— Male animals should have two apparently normal testicles fully descended into the scrotum.

The well-muscled hindquarters of WildWind's Day Dream Fantasy, two-year-old bitch by Ch. Tara's Doc Holiday ex Sirius Cleopatra. Bred and owned by Chet and Lauraine Rodgers.

Above: A portrait of the colorful family of Evergreen Am. Staffs. Left to right, Wheezer's Shady Lady; Ch. Ringo; Am., Can. Ch. Demon Seed; Ch. Belle; and Ch. Sunny. Owned by Jim and Carolyn Brown. *Below:* Cresstock Our Lady Goldberry, by Ch. Reetun's Red Tornado ex Ch. Cresstock's Delight, bred by Bonnie Cresse, owned by Lorraine Richards of Salt Lake City, UT. This excellent bitch has done well with Best-of-Breed and Best-of-Opposite-Sex wins from the classes.

Colors and Movement: Staffordshire Bull Terrier

By John H. Martin, D.V.M.

The color clue in Staffordshires is much misunderstood. The blue gene seems to be a simple recessive and may appear as solid blue, blue brindle, or blue-fawn. The last color is marked like the masked fawns, except the points are blue instead of black. All of the blues that I have seen in either Staffordshire Bull Terriers or American Staffordshire Terriers have dark blue noses and eye rims. Since this is a dilute color, it seems that true black does not come with it, but blue from medium to very dark. Usually the eye color is somewhat dilute, making the eyes a bit lighter than one would wish. The blues, particularly the blue-fawns, have upon occasion been confused with or mistaken for liver. If one has seen a real liver dog, discerning the difference is easy. Livers are usually solid of that color, possibly marked with white, have brown noses and brown—not blue—eye rims. A good look at an English Springer Spaniel of the liver and white color combination, or a liver-spotted Pointer, or a Sussex or Field Spaniel will give one a clear impression of the true liver color.

Black and tan, the other disqualified color, also confuses some folks. They speak of tri-colors when the black and tan is marked with white. In my opinion, any dog of the black and tan pattern (marked with tan in the same pattern as the black and tan breeds such as Doberman Pinschers and Manchester Terriers) is a black and tan dog in the meaning of the standard. Some of the confusion is due to the fact that while these colors in Staffordshire Bull Terriers call for complete disqualification, with American Staffordshire Terriers the standard states

Gait is defined as "the pattern of footsteps at various rates of speed, each pattern distinguished by a particular rhythm and footfall. The two gaits acceptable in the show ring are the walk and trot."

These two Staffordshire Bull Terriers illustrate the two color disqualifications in the breed and colors "not to be encouraged" in American Staffordshire Terriers. The black and tan SBT speaks for itself, a pattern akin to that of Dobermans or Manchester Terriers. The liver-colored SBT here is a paler shade, as darker livers occur also; this coloration is instantly identifiable by the liver-colored eye rims and nose leather as well as the light-colored eyes.

merely that these colors are not to be encouraged. I know of a couple of American Staffordshire champions that are black and tan. I feel that the awarding of points to such specimens might be interpreted as encouragement.

ACTION IN THE STAFFORDSHIRE BULL TERRIER

The standard for Staffordshire Bull Terriers makes no mention of gait. However, it does give a clear picture of the desired structure and conformation of the breed. Anyone with a real understanding of gait in either dogs or horses knows that an animal must move in

accordance with the way he is put together. We are dealing with a rather "squatty" dog of fair bone and heavy musculature, wide and deep in the chest and with a deep, well-sprung rib cage.

Both the shoulders and hips must show very pronounced muscling. While both front and hind legs should be parallel, the front feet turn out a little below the pasterns. Here is a dog that in another type terrier might be called "loaded in the shoulder" and "with turned out front feet." This sort of dog cannot move as clean as a Fox Terrier or an Airedale, as he is not built to do so. He should move straight ahead with fair freedom of action, but the feet are inclined to paddle a bit in front due to the dog's structure.

Hind legs should move true, but due to his width the dog will tend to move his feet more toward the center line as his speed increases. This is necessary for him to balance himself.

The thing that I most abhor is a dog who is stiff behind due to lack of angulation. You can have this lack in both the stifle and the hocks.

How many times I have seen otherwise knowledgeable judges attempt to straighten the front feet when a Stafford is stacked for examination! Remember, this is a different type of terrier from most. You are not looking for speed, but for a dog showing great strength for his size, so he has to move differently.

Ch. Guardstock's Red Atom being exercised by Bill Daniels. Atom's favorite exercise: holding on to his leash with his mouth, and playing "ring around the rosie."

The Purchase of Your Staffordshire

Careful consideration should be given to what breed of dog you wish to own prior to your purchase of one. If several breeds are attractive to you, and you are undecided as to which you prefer, learn all you can about the characteristics of each before making your decision. As you do so, you are thus preparing yourself to make an intelligent choice; and this is very important when buying a dog who will be, with reasonable luck, a member of your household for at least a dozen years or more. Obviously, since you are reading this book, you have decided on the breed—so now all that remains is to make a good choice.

It is never wise to just rush out and buy the first cute puppy who catches your eye. Whether you wish a dog to show, one with whom to compete in obedience, or one as a family dog purely for his (or her) companionship, the more time and thought you invest as you plan the purchase, the more likely you are to meet with complete satisfaction. The background and early care behind your pet will reflect in the dog's future health and temperament. Even if you are planning the purchase purely as a pet, with no thoughts of showing or breeding in the dog's or puppy's future, it is essential that, if the dog is to enjoy a trouble-free future, you assure yourself of a healthy, properly raised puppy or adult from sturdy, well-bred stock.

Throughout the pages of this book you will find the names and locations of many well-known and well-established kennels in various areas. Another source of information is the American Kennel Club (51 Madison Avenue, New York, New York 10010), from whom you can obtain a list of recognized breeders in the vicinity of your home. If you plan to have your dog

Opposite: **Ch. Barzak's Lady Winfred, C.D., a fine SBT owned by Judy Keller.**

campaigned by a professional handler, by all means let the handler help you locate and select a good dog. Through their numerous clients, handlers have access to a variety of interesting show prospects; and the usual arrangement is that the handler re-sells the dog to you for what his cost has been, with the agreement that the dog be campaigned for you by him throughout the dog's career. It is most strongly recommended that prospective purchasers follow these suggestions, as you thus will be better able to locate and select a satisfactory puppy or dog.

Your first step in searching for your puppy is to make appointments at kennels specializing in your breed, where you can visit and inspect the dogs, both those available for sale and the kennel's basic breeding stock. You are looking for an active, sturdy puppy with bright eyes and intelligent expression and who is friendly and alert; avoid puppies who are hyperactive, dull, or listless. The coat should be clean and thick, with no sign of parasites. The premises on which he was raised should look (and smell) clean and be tidy, making it obvious that the puppies and their surroundings are in capable hands. Should the kennels featuring the breed you intend to own be sparse in your area or not have what you consider attractive, do not hesitate to contact others at a distance and purchase from them if they seem better able to supply a puppy or dog who will please you—*so long as it is a recognized breeding kennel of that*

Am Staff pups "April" and "Kea" in the hands of breeder Ernest Prehn.

breed. Shipping dogs is a regular practice nowadays, with comparatively few problems when one considers the number of dogs shipped each year. A reputable, well-known breeder wants the customer to be satisfied; thus, he will represent the puppy fairly. Should you not be pleased with the puppy upon arrival, a breeder, such as described, will almost certainly permit its return. A conscientious breeder takes real interest and concern in the welfare of the dogs he or she causes to be brought into the world. Such a breeder also is proud of a reputation for integrity. Thus on two counts,

This is Cock 'N' Bull Kennels' Roses are Red, a handsome uncropped American Staffordshire Terrier.

Eng. Ch. Ben Hur and "Motley" the cat are owned by Mr. R. Austin.

for the sake of the dog's future and the breeder's reputation, to such a person a *satisfied* customer takes precedence over a sale at any cost.

If your puppy is to be a pet or "family dog," the earlier the age at which it joins your household the better. Puppies are weaned and ready to start out on their own, under the care of a sensible new owner, at about six weeks old; and if you take a young one, it is often easier to train it to the routine of your household and to your requirements of it than is the case with an older dog which, even though still technically a puppy, may have already started habits you will find difficult to change. The younger puppy is usually less costly, too, as it stands to reason the breeder will not have as much expense invested in it. Obviously, a puppy that has been raised to five or six

months old represents more in care and cash expenditure on the breeder's part than one sold earlier; therefore he should be, and generally is, priced accordingly.

There is an enormous amount of truth in the statement that "bargain" puppies seldom turn out to be that. A "cheap" puppy, raised purely for sale and profit, can and often does lead to great heartbreak, including problems and veterinarian's bills which can add up to many times the initial cost of a properly reared dog. On the other hand, just because a puppy is expensive does not assure one that it is healthy and well reared. There have been numerous cases where unscrupulous dealers have sold, for several hundred dollars, puppies that were sickly, in poor condition, and such poor specimens that the breed of which they were supposedly members was barely recognizable. So one cannot always judge a puppy by price alone. Common sense must guide a prospective purchaser, plus the selection of a *reliable,* well-recommended dealer whom you know to have well-satisfied customers or, best of all, a specialized breeder. You will probably find the fairest pricing at the kennel of a breeder. Such a person, experienced with the breed in general and with his or her own stock in particular, through extensive association with these dogs, has watched enough of them mature to have obviously learned to assess quite accurately each puppy's potential—something impossible where such background is non-existent.

One more word on the subject of pets. Bitches make a fine choice for this purpose as they are usually quieter and more gentle than the males, easier to house train, more affectionate, and less inclined to roam. If you do select a bitch and have no intention of breeding or showing her, by all means have her spayed, for your sake and for hers. The advantages to the owner of a spayed bitch include avoiding the nuisance of "in season" periods which normally occur twice yearly—with the accompanying eager canine swains haunting your premises in an effort to get close to your female—plus the unavoidable messiness and spotting of

furniture and rugs at this time, which can be annoying if she is a household companion in the habit of sharing your sofa or bed. As for the spayed bitch, she benefits as she grows older because this simple operation almost entirely eliminates the possibility of breast cancer ever occurring. It is recommended that all bitches eventually be spayed—even those used for show or breeding when their careers have ended—in order that they may enjoy a happier, healthier old age. Please take note, however, that a bitch who has been spayed (or an altered dog) *cannot be shown at American Kennel Club dog shows once this operation has been performed*. Be certain that you are *not* interested in showing her before taking this step.

Also, in selecting a pet, never underestimate the advantages of an older dog, perhaps a retired

A litter of American Staffordshire Terriers owned by Karen Tucker.

show dog or a bitch no longer needed for breeding, who may be available and quite reasonably priced by a breeder anxious to place such a dog in a loving home. These dogs are settled and can be a delight to own, as they make wonderful companions, especially in a household of adults where raising a puppy can sometimes be a trial.

Everything that has been said about careful selection of your pet puppy and its place of purchase applies, but with many further considerations, when you plan to buy a show dog or foundation stock for a future breeding program. Now is the time for an in-depth study of the breed, starting with every word and every illustration in this book and all others you can find written on the subject. The Standard of the breed has now become your guide, and you must learn not only the words but also how to interpret them and how to apply them to actual dogs before you are ready to make an

Who could resist so appealing a puppy as this young Stafford? Scalliwag of Cresstock, by Reetun's Rufus The Red ex Ch. Cresstock Our Tawny was bred by Bonnie Cresse and belongs to Pete Reid.

intelligent selection of a show dog.

If you are thinking in terms of a dog to show, obviously you must have learned about dog shows and must be in the habit of attending them. This is fine, but now your activity in this direction should be increased, with your attending every single dog show within a reasonable distance from your home. Much can be learned about a breed at ringside at these events. Talk with the breeders who are exhibiting. Study the dogs they are showing. Watch the judging with concentration, noting each decision made, and attempt to follow the reasoning by which the judge has reached it. Note carefully the attributes of the dogs who win and, for your later use, the manner in which each is presented. Close your ears to the ringside know-it-alls, usually novice owners of a dog or two and very new to the Fancy, who have only derogatory remarks to make about all that is taking place unless they happen to win. This is the type of exhibitor who "comes and goes" through the Fancy and whose interest is usually of very short duration, owing to lack of knowledge and dissatisfaction caused by the failure to recognize the need to learn. You, as a fancier whom we hope will last and enjoy our sport over many future years, should develop independent thinking at this stage; you should learn to draw your own conclusions about the merits, or lack of them, seen before you in the ring and, thus, sharpen your own judgement in preparation for choosing wisely and well.

Note carefully which breeders campaign winning dogs—not just an occasional isolated good one, but representative kennels raising this breed within a reasonable distance. If so, by all means ask permission of the owners to visit the kennels and do so when permission is granted. You may not necessarily buy then and there, as they may not have available what you are

consistent, homebred winners. It is from one of these people that you should select your own future "star."

If you are located in an area where dog shows take place only occasionally or where there are long travel distances involved, you will need to find another testing ground for your ability to select a worthy show dog. Possibly, there are some seeking that very day, but you will be able to see the type of dog being raised there and to discuss the dogs with the breeder. Every time you do this, you add to your knowledge. Should one of these kennels have dogs which especially appeal to you, perhaps you could reserve a show-prospect puppy from a coming litter. This is frequently

A beguiling SBT pup owned by Judy Keller, this is future Ch. Lady Barzak's Lady Winfred, C.D. Age: three and a half months.

Top: Goldwyn Golden Lad is an SBT co-owned by M.J. Wall and J.A. Altoft.
Bottom: Ch. Normandie Lady of Shars shown finishing at nine months with her fifth major. Owner-handled by Jeanne Pierrette Dross.

English Ch. Goldwyn Lucky Star, a Staffordshire Bull Terrier owned by Peter and Sheila Wall of Travwall Kennels.

done, and it is often worth waiting for a puppy, unless you have seen a dog with which you truly are greatly impressed and which is immediately available.

The purchase of a puppy has already been discussed. Obviously this same approach applies in a far greater degree when the purchase involved is a future show dog. The only place from which to purchase a show prospect is a breeder who raises show-type stock;

Sooner's Mac Attack, by Ch. Sooner's Big Mac ex Ch. Nugent's Merry Midnight, C.D., pictured at age five months. Bred by Lois Smith. A most endearing puppy.

otherwise, you are almost certainly doomed to disappointment as the puppy matures. Show and breeding kennels obviously cannot keep all of their fine young stock. An active breeder-exhibitor is, therefore, happy to place promising youngsters in the hands of people also interested in showing and winning with them, doing so at a fair price according to the quality and prospects of the dog involved. Here again, if no kennel in your immediate area has what you are seeking, do not hesitate to contact top breeders in other areas and to buy at long distance. Ask for pictures, pedigrees, and a complete description. Heed the breeder's advice and recommendations, after truthfully telling exactly what your expectations are for the dog you purchase. Do you want something with which to win just a few ribbons now and then? Do you want a dog who can complete his championship? Are you thinking of the real "big time" (*i.e.*, seriously campaigning with Best of Breed, Group wins, and possibly even Best in Show as your eventual goal)? Consider it all carefully in advance; then honestly discuss your plans with the breeder. You will be better satisfied with the results if you do this, as the breeder is then in the best position to help you choose the dog who is most likely to come through for you. A breeder selling a show dog is just as anxious as the buyer for the dog to succeed, and the breeder will represent the dog to you with truth and honesty. Also, this type of breeder does not lose interest the moment the sale has been made but, when necessary, will be right there to assist you with beneficial advice and suggestions based on years of experience.

As you make inquiries of at least several kennels, keep in mind that show-prospect puppies are less expensive than mature show dogs, the latter often costing close to four figures, and sometimes more.

Ch. Patton's Smoki Topaz, owned by Cock 'N' Bull Kennels. This lovely bitch, the dam of Ch. Oltyme's Cock O' The Walk, is a granddaughter of Ch. White Rock Jet Bomber, Ch. Atchley's Fanny, Ch. Patton's Pagan Piglet Laws and Ch. Patton's Wildfire of Harber, C.D., A blue fawn male owned by Jerry Brown.

The reason for this is that, with a puppy, there is always an element of chance, the possibility of it's developing unexpected faults as it matures or failing to develop the excellence and quality that earlier had seemed probable. There definitely is a risk factor in buying a show-prospect puppy. Sometimes all goes well, but occasionally the swan becomes an ugly duckling. Reflect on this as you consider available puppies and young adults. It just might be a good idea to go with a more mature, though more costly, dog if one you like is available.

When you buy a mature show dog, "what you see is what you get," and it is not likely to change beyond coat and condition, which are dependent on your care. Also advantageous for a novice owner is the fact that a mature dog of show quality almost certainly will have received show-ring training and probably match-show experience, which will make your earliest handling ventures much easier.

Frequently it is possible to purchase a beautiful dog who has completed championship but who, owing to similarity in bloodlines, is not needed for the breeder's future program. Here you have the opportunity of owning a champion, usually in the two-to-five-year-old range, which you can enjoy campaigning as a special (for Best of Breed competition) and which will be a settled, handsome dog for you and your family to enjoy with pride.

If you are planning foundation for a future kennel, concentrate on acquiring one or two really superior bitches. These need not be top show-quality, but they should represent your breed's finest producing bloodlines from a strain noted for producing quality, generation after generation. A proven matron who is already the dam of show-type puppies is, of course, the ideal selection; but these are usually difficult to obtain, no one being anxious to part with so valuable an asset. You just might strike it lucky, though, in which case you are off to a flying start. If you cannot find such a matron available, select a young bitch of finest background from top-producing lines who is herself of decent type, free of obvious faults, and of good quality.

Great attention should be paid to the pedigree of the bitch from whom you intend to breed. If not already known to

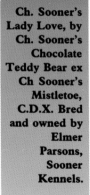

Ch. Sooner's Lady Love, by Ch. Sooner's Chocolate Teddy Bear ex Ch Sooner's Mistletoe, C.D.X. Bred and owned by Elmer Parsons, Sooner Kennels.

you, try to see the sire and dam. It is generally agreed that someone starting with a breed should concentrate on a fine collection of topflight bitches and raise a few litters from these before considering keeping one's own stud dog. The practice of buying a stud and then breeding everything you own or acquire to that dog does not always work out well. It is better to take advantage of the many noted sires who are available to be used at stud, who represent all of the leading strains, and, in each case, to carefully select the one who in type and pedigree seems most compatible to each of your bitches, at least for your first several litters.

To summarize, if you want a "family dog" as a companion, it is best to buy it young and raise it according to the habits of your household. If you are buying a show dog, the more mature it is, the more certain you can be of its future beauty. If you are buying foundation stock for a kennel, then bitches are better, but they must be from the finest *producing* bloodlines.

When you buy a pure-bred dog that you are told is eligible for registration with the American Kennel Club, you are entitled to receive from the

Chester and Lauraine Rodgers's Am Staff urchins: WildWinds Butch Cassidy and WildWinds Bella Donna.

Ch Steeltown's Blue Monday, owned by Cock 'N' Bull Kennels, is another famous American Staffordshire who devotes time to working with therapy patients, doing so through the Humane Society's Animal Facilitated Therapy Program. Blue Monday's owners, Dr. Jerry E. and Julianna A. Brown, feel that this participation is Blue Monday's finest achievement.

seller an application form which will enable you to register your dog. If the seller cannot give you the application form, you should demand and receive an identification of your dog, consisting of the name of the breed, the registered names and numbers of the sire and dam, the name of the breeder, and your dog's date of birth. If the litter of which your dog is a part is already recorded with the American Kennel Club, then the litter number is sufficient identification.

Do not be misled by promises of papers at some later date. Demand a registration application form or proper identification as described above. If neither is supplied, do not buy the dog. So warns the American Kennel Club, and this is especially important in the purchase of show or breeding stock.

OWNING A STAFFORDSHIRE

First and foremost, the Staffordshire breeds are family dogs. They are never happier than when with the humans they love. Quiet, neat, and not destructive, they make fabulous house dogs. They make outstanding city dogs, where their protective instincts are put to good use. The apartment guarded by a Staffordshire is in capable paws, as is the owner when accompanied by a Staff on city streets.

They also excel as farm dogs, giving sensible and quick protection from marauders as they protect the livestock and, being terriers, hold down the vermin population.

The suburbs probably pose the greatest problem for these

dogs, who are not suited to being turned loose to roam at large. Of course, all dogs should be kept in fenced areas on their owner's property, but this is especially important in the case of a Staffordshire. It is their nature never to refuse the challenge of another dog. Such an altercation is hardly desirable and therefore should be avoided. Responsible Staffordshire owners fence in their yards, or an area of them; and their dogs, accompanied by an adult family member are walked on leads for further exercise and relaxation.

Raised with children, Staffordshires are deep in their devotion and concern. Endless stories have been told about the occasions on which a Staff has saved "his" youngster from accident, danger, and attack from vicious dogs of other breeds. Staffordshires will play for hours at a time, never seeming to tire, then curl up to nap with the youngster.

Being quiet and not given to senseless barking, Staffordshires make extremely effective guard dogs. The knowledge of one's being present on the premises is a cautionary note to thieves and others with criminal intent who stand in awe of the breed. One can feel quite safe, at home or abroad, in the company of a Staffordshire.

Despite the breed's self-reliance and rugged appearance, these dogs are babies at heart, thoroughly enjoying all the comforts of home, petting, and lots of human companionship. They get along well with other household pets, too, if the introduction is made tactfully and at an early age. Most will welcome a puppy or kitten into the household, and the two will quickly become friends.

If you live in the city, this does not preclude the owning of a Staffordshire. They are not too large to be apartment dogs, although they do need to be taken on a couple of walks a day in addition to "quick trips to the curb." Walking in the city can be fun and healthful, especially with an "on the job" guardian at your side to protect you.

Staffordshire owners are so completely satisfied with their dogs that not even for a moment could they be persuaded to switch their interest to another breed. They look at you in horror should you make such a suggestion, as they know—having experienced it—that a Staffordshire is second to none in one's household.

This has been a difficult period for the Staffordshire breeds and even more so for the people who love them. The press and television media, triggered by some unfortunate instances, have been conducting a vendetta against any kind of dog even faintly resembling the "pit bull." Lurid stories and headlines have flashed on the television screen and in newspapers. True, sensationalism is the

"Staffordshire owners are so completely satisfied with their dogs that not even for a moment could they be persuaded to switch their interest to another breed."

Cock 'N' Bull's Violets Are Blue, sired by Blue Monday, was bred by Cock 'N' Bull Kennels.

lifeblood of these people, but in this instance it seems to many of us that they have gone a bit "beyond the call of duty" in recording some instances of dogs who have bitten or attacked people.

It should not be forgotten that dogs of *any* breed will bite if provoked. It is not a sign of viciousness if a dog turns on a child or adult who is in some manner tormenting that dog. Patience in an animal can be stretched only so far before it reaches the breaking point. (Actually, Staffordshires have far more endurance than many breeds and greater tolerance to pain.)

Also, a watchdog on duty cannot be blamed for attacking what appears to be an intruder. After all, that is what one *expects* and *wants* of a guard dog. If someone owning a dog permits a friend or acquaintance to enter an area where the dog is on guard, is it not the owner's fault, rather than the dog's, if the animal attacks that person who seems to be intruding? To my way of thinking it is!

Staffordshire owners, like the owners of any powerful breed of dog, have certain obligations to their dog and to their community. No Staffordshire should ever be permitted to roam at large. The "enjoyment of his freedom," as some dog owners call it, is actually irresponsibility on the part of the owner and a tremendous disservice to the breed and to the individual dog. Be mindful of the well-known dangers for dogs out on their own, which include being hit by a car (to be killed, or even worse, left alive and suffering along the roadside) and being stolen. The Staffordshire breeds are in special danger here, as many are picked up on the street by thieves, or even snatched from the parked car or fenced yard of the owner, sometimes right in front of the owner. The person committing such an act hopes the dog can be trained for dog fighting or some other illegal purpose. All the publicity given by the news media can make these practices seem very tempting to certain groups of people in today's world.

So, be a *responsible* dog owner and protect your dog by proper precautions. A Staffordshire who is stolen seldom gets back home again and almost certainly will come to no good end—hardly the fate your gentle, well-loved pet deserves.

AMERICAN STAFFORDSHIRE OWNERS TALK OF THEIR BREED

Such a lot of talk has gone around lately on the subject of the temperament of Staffordshires that we have

Ch. Sooner's Boomer Sooner, by Ch. Ruffian Little T of Har-Wyn. Bred by Lois Smith, owned by Olivia Patterson, who is handling him to a Terrier Group Second. This dog was Winners Dog at the 1975 National Specialty, a Top Ten "Special," and No. 1 All-Systems, for 1979. A Top Producer, this is the grandsire of Ch. S'N'S Ogre Easy.

Top: Top Sire in Am Staff history, and holder of the world record for weight pull, at a height of 20 inches and weight of 68 pounds, Ch. Tryarr's Diamond-back Redbolt with his handler John C. McCartney winning Best of Breed in 1980.
Bottom: The famous "Dagmar," Ch. Fraja's Thunder Battery, taking Best of Breed at Westchester in 1981. Bred by Sue Ann Thompson. Owned and handled by John C. McCartney. Dagmar is an outstanding show bitch and the dam of several champions.

Top: Kodiak's Windrider, by Ch. Aranda Angelina V. Kodiak ex Ch. Byron's Finn McCool, pictured winning Best of Winners at one year of age in 1986. *Bottom:* Ch. Iron Buck's Painted Tart, C.D., owned by James D. Wheat.

127

We love this photo of Ch. Kingsblood Royal Val, grand matriarch of the Doc's Staffordshire Bull Terriers, napping with her new charge, Dr. Martin's beautiful little English Toy Spaniel, who seems to think that Val is her grandmother. As Dr. Martin says, "If you have no children for them to look after, they will adopt a puppy." Val is 12 years old in this photo.

decided to bring you a special section on this subject, presenting opinions of those best acquainted with and thus best qualified to discuss the character and behavior patterns of this breed. The comments presented are from people who know Staffordshires, have lived with these dogs, and owned and raised them. Who better to speak of the Staffordshire's qualifications as a family dog?

Recently, at a dog show, I had the pleasure of meeting Pamela Scariato from Matamoras, Pennsylvania, who

words, "I was parked in front of an ice cream parlor when a man pulled up in a pickup truck, and in the back was this big red dog, with such character in his face and a lively gleam in his eye. I got out of my car and walked up to the man and asked a few questions about this beautiful dog with rippling muscles and his ready love for humans of any size. After awhile I asked if he would sell me this dog, and to my surprise the man asked how much I had, to which I quickly replied $98.00, which is a lot of

has been an Am Staff owner for ten years and truly loves the breed. Pamela recalls watching the *Our Gang* comedies and asking her father to please find her a dog like "Pete." It was not until she had reached age 16 that she finally found the dog of her dreams.

To tell you in Pamela's own

money in the dead of winter in West Virginia when the coal miners are on strike." Pamela's offer was, of course, accepted, and Fred, as the dog was called, is now 13 years old and living with her father in West Virginia.

Pamela and Daniel Scariato now own another big red dog.

Ch. Diamonds Hot Wax of Sans Tache, Top American Staffordshire Terrier Bitch for 1984, *Canine Chronicle* System. By Ch. Trgarr Diamondback Red Bolt ex Ch. Tryarr Diamonds Are Forever. "Sweet Pea" here is at a very young age and already winning Group placements. Her show career was a short one as she was only campaigned over a four-month period, but her impact on the fancy was tremendous, with many experts considering her to be among the most outstanding bitches the breed has known. Owner, Joe LeBlanc. Handler, Fred Sindelar.

He is rapidly earning a reputation for himself as Champion Ryan's D.J., a successful winning contender in the show ring in the keenest high quality competition. This is by no means D.J.'s only claim to fame however, for he puts in a full work week between dog shows, visiting sixteen patients twice weekly in a trauma center, plus his other calls.

D.J.'s patients range in age from 15 to 65 years, and the doctors are truly amazed at the tremendous progress this superb dog has made with some of them. It is explained that such patients will sometimes relate to animals far more quickly than they will to people—which is where D.J. enters the picture.

Again quoting Pamela, "Staffs make great therapy dogs because of their almost human abilities and great tolerance for pain. We often will have a patient who takes his frustration out on D.J. with no warning whatsoever by kicking or hitting him. D.J. will just stand there as though to say 'I understand. This person doesn't mean any harm really'."

D.J. is also off-lead obedience trained. Daniel Scariato could even take him to a dog show and work him off-lead and he would never go for another dog.

As for children, D.J. is the

greatest for taking his owners' 19-month-old son on rides around the house and exchanging licks on that ice cream cone which he feels is far too big for little Nick to eat all by himself. When night comes and all kisses and hugs are given, he scurries upstairs with the Scariatos' five-year-old daughter, April, with whom he sleeps.

D.J. visits schools for retarded children as well as public schools where again he demonstrates his gentle nature.

This handsome youngster is Cock 'N' Bull's Talk A Blue Streak, a son of the great Ch. Steeltown's Blue Monday. Owners, Dr. Jerry E. Brown and Julianna A. Brown.

The Scariatos also have six bitches who live with them, all of which are great, too. Whenever a litter is born, D.J. waits patiently for the chance to jump into the whelping box and help tend to his puppies—when mom is outside, of course—by licking them gently and letting them teethe on his face.

Pamela Scariato continues, "Let's talk a little about breeding. When I started as a breeder, I did not breed for conformation, I bred for temperament and stability. I had no idea then that I would ever walk into the show ring and do with my dogs what I have done. All I knew was that my dogs were sound in body and their best quality couldn't be seen by a jaunt around the show ring.

"D.J. finished in his first four or five shows with four 'majors' and four Bests of Breed over 'specials.' He has ranked No. 1 in the U.S. for breed points, No. 4 in Group systems, and is No. 48 among all Terriers. But more important, he is No. 1 in the hearts of so many people that he gives his consistent love and devotion, his comfort in times of sadness, his caring in times of stress, his quiet way of always letting his people know 'I am here'."

Carolyn Brown of Evergreen Staffordshires also speaks with very evident love of the Staffordshire breed. She mentions their adaptability to situations, even, as she says, to the point of hurting one's feelings. "Wheezer," one of her favorites, had gone to live with a friend of Carolyn's. It was a hard decision for her to make, but she knew that this would be an ideal home for him. When it came time for her to leave without him, it was hard for her to do so. Wheezer on the other hand, who had been inspecting the premises with obvious satisfaction, had confidence in Mrs. Brown having done well by him in the selection of a new home. His good-bye as she left was what she describes as "his gorgeous look" as he turned to continue inspection of the premises. He and his new mom became familiar figures in the neighborhood. They daily walk through the streets and are invited into all the stores for conversation and petting, to Wheezer's obvious enjoyment.

Carolyn Brown speaks, too, of Shady, who is a bit of an escape artist, loving to jump the fence to the yard where all the neighborhood kids play. Twice the Browns have found her playing ball with the kids, because they had a ball and because that is her favorite toy. Shady is also an excellent protector. Jim Brown, Carolyn's husband, brought his business partner home one evening to wait while he changed for bowling. The partner waited downstairs, and Shady felt obligated to keep an eye on him until her master returned. Each time the partner moved to the right or to the left—or anywhere at all—Shady moved right along with him, then sat down. The Browns heard an appeal from downstairs to "please come," and the moment Jim showed up, all was well. Shady and Jim's business partner became fast friends after that. In fact, she slept at the foot of the bed that night when he stayed over.

Ch. Ledge Rock's Blue Velvet and feline friend snapped at home in 1986. Ernest and Ruth Prehn, owners, Ledge Rock Kennels.

Top: Best of Breed and Best of Opposite Sex, Ch. Ledge Rock's Kopper Korn and Ch. Ledge Rock's Lucy in the Sky, bred by Ernest and Ruth Prehn and owned by Joye Lucarelli and Ruth Prehn.
Center: Champion WildWind's Apache Brave, by Ch. Sooner's True Grit of Rhody ex Ch. Tex-Rock Queen of Diamonds, and WildWind's Sweet Chevron, by Ch. Sooner's True Grit of Rody ex Sirius Cleopatra. Bred and owned by Chet and Lauraine Rodgers.
Bottom: Dagmar, a black-brindle and white Am Staff owned by John C. McCartney, taking Best of Breed, owner-handled.

An awesome Staffordshire Bull Terrier in breed history, Eng., Am., Can., and Mex. Ch. Reetun's Lord Jim, handled by Wood Wornall for owner J. Zane Smith to a Group first under the author.

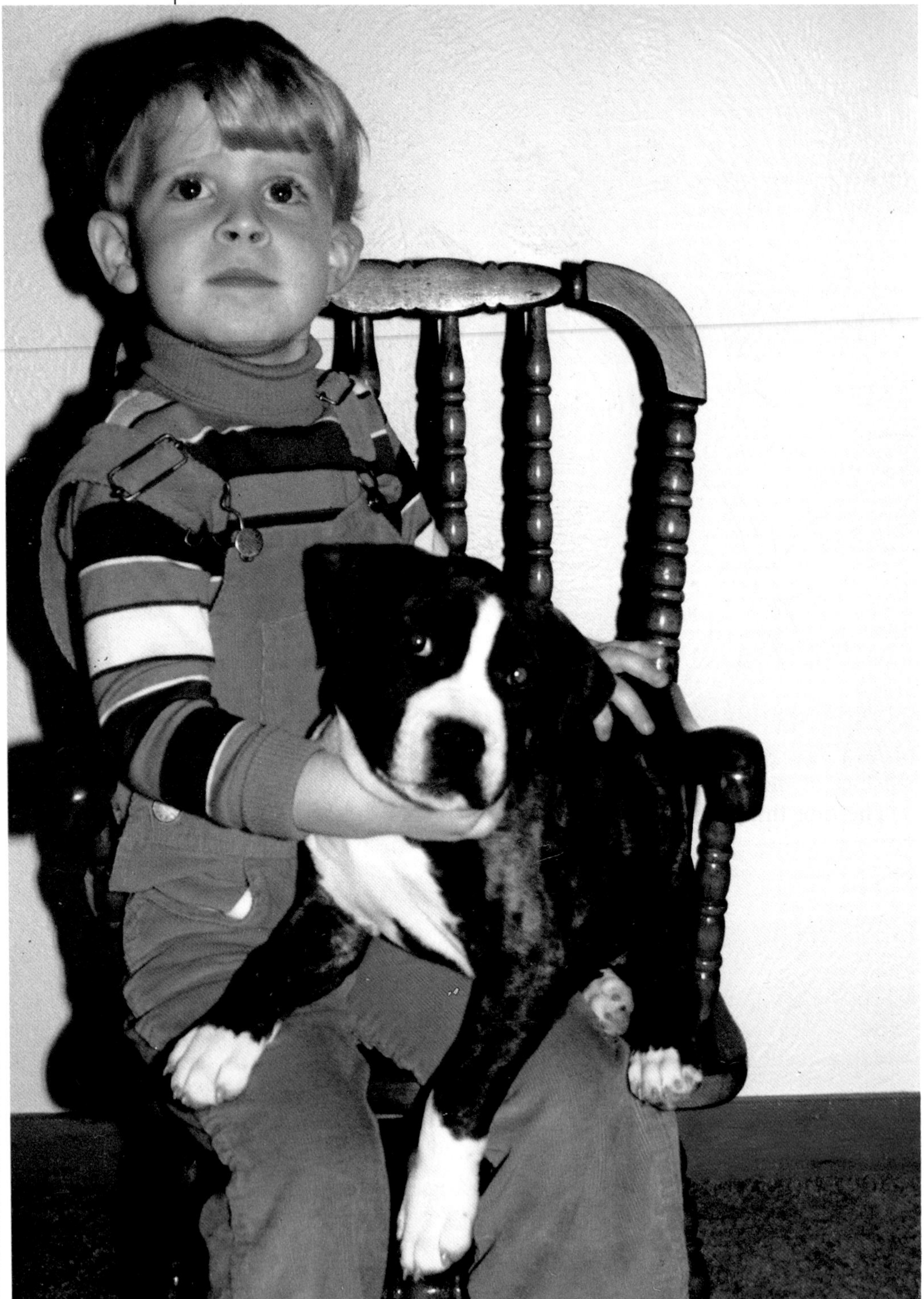

The Care of Your Staffordshire Puppy

The moment you decide to be the new owner of a puppy is not one second too soon to start planning for the puppy's arrival in your home. Both the new family member and you will find the transition period easier if your home is geared in advance of the arrival.

The first things to be prepared are a bed for the puppy and a place where you can pen him up for rest periods. Every dog should have a crate of its own from the very beginning, so that he will come to know and love it as his special place where he is safe and happy. It is an ideal arrangement, for when you want him to be free, the crate stays open. At other times you can securely latch it and know that the pup is safely out of mischief. If you travel with him, his crate comes along in the car; and, of course, in traveling by plane there is no alternative but to have a carrier for the dog. If you show your

dog, you will want him upon occasion to be in a crate a good deal of the day. So from every consideration, a crate is a very sensible and sound investment in your puppy's future safety and happiness and for your own peace of mind.

The crates most desirable are the sturdy plastic ones with removable side panels, which are ideal for cold weather (with the panels in place to keep out drafts) and in hot weather (with the panels removed to allow better air circulation). Wire crates are all right in the summer, but they give no protection from cold or drafts. Aluminum crates, due to the manner in which the metal reflects surrounding temperatures, are not recommended. If it is cold, so is the metal of the crate; if it is hot, the crate becomes burning hot.

When you choose the puppy's crate, be certain that it is roomy enough not to become

Opposite:
Eddie Wick with his pal Ledge Rock's Cherokee Fiddler, owned by Pat and Paul Wick.

Lunchtime and the eager babies each crowd around to get its share. Photo, Karen Tucker.

Ch. Willynwood Velvet Shadow with puppy, Ledge Rock's Victor. Two of the delightful Am Staffs belonging to Ernest and Ruth Prehn.

outgrown. The crate should have sufficient height so the dog can stand up in it as a mature dog and sufficient area so that he can stretch out full length when relaxed. When the puppy is young, first give him shredded newspaper as a bed; the papers can be replaced with a mat or turkish towels when the dog is older. Carpet remnants are great for the bottom of the crate, as they are inexpensive and in case of accidents can be quite easily replaced. As the dog matures and is past the chewing age, a pillow or blanket in the crate is an appreciated comfort.

Sharing importance with the crate is a safe area in which the puppy can exercise and play. If you are an apartment dweller, a baby's playpen works out well for a young dog; for an older puppy use a portable exercise pen which you can use later when travelling with your dog or for dog shows. If you have a

yard, an area where he can be outside in safety should be fenced in prior to the dog's arrival at your home. This area does not need to be huge, but it does need to be made safe and secure. If you are in a suburban area where there are close neighbors, stockade fencing works out best, as then the neighbors are less aware of the dog and the dog cannot see and bark at everything passing by.

If you are out in the country where no problems with neighbors are likely to occur, then regular chain-link fencing is fine. For added precaution in both cases, use a row of concrete blocks or railroad ties inside against the entire bottom of the fence; this precludes or at least considerably lessens the chances of your dog digging his way out.

extremely important to a puppy's muscular development and to keep a mature dog fit and trim. So make sure that those exercise periods, or walks, a game of ball, and other such activities, are part of your daily program as a dog owner.

If your fenced area has an outside gate, provide a padlock and key and a strong fastening for it, and use them, so that the

Ch. Cock 'N' Bull's Johnny Walker, a homebred SBT owned by Cock 'N' Bull Kennels, CA, a kennel dedicated to the interest of all Staff breeds.

Be advised that if yours is a single dog, it is very unlikely that it will get sufficient exercise just sitting in the fenced area, which is what most of them do when they are there alone. Two or more dogs will play and move themselves around, but one by itself does little more than make a leisurely tour once around the area to check things over and then lie down. You must include a daily walk or two in your plans if your puppy is to be rugged and well. Exercise is

gate cannot be opened by others and the dog taken or turned free. The ultimate convenience in this regard is, of course, a door (unused for other purposes) from the house around which the fenced area can be enclosed, so that all you have to do is open the door and out into his area he goes. This arrangement is safest of all, as then you need not be using a gate, and it is easier in bad weather since then you can send the dog out without taking him and becoming soaked

Ch. Cerberus's Pecan Poko, by Ch. Sligo McCarthy ex Prizer The Scarlet Fire Fox. This handsome young bitch is pictured winning a Group placement at New Brunswick K.C. in 1986, under expert Ron Krohne. Pecan Poko was bred by C. Filipos and R. Croll; she is owned by Rita and Tony Pauciello of Hopatcong, NJ.

yourself at the same time. This is not always possible to manage, but if your house is arranged so that you could do it this way, you would never regret it due to the convenience and added safety thus provided. Fencing in the entire yard, with gates to be opened and closed whenever a caller, deliveryman, postman, or some other person comes on your property, really is not safe at all because people not used to gates are frequently careless about closing and latching them *securely*. Many heartbreaking incidents have been brought about by someone carelessly half closing a gate (which the owner had thought to be firmly latched) and the dog wandering out. For greatest security a fenced *area*

definitely takes precedence over a fenced *yard*.

The puppy will need a collar (one that fits now, not one to be grown into) and a lead from the moment you bring him home. Both should be an appropriate weight and type for his size. Also needed are a feeding dish and a water dish, both made preferably of unbreakable material. Your pet supply shop should have an interesting assortment of these and other accessories from which you can choose. Then you will need grooming tools of the type the breeder recommends and some toys. Equally satisfactory is Nylabone®, a nylon bone that does not chip or splinter and that "frizzles" as the puppy chews, providing healthful gum

Ch. What A Classy Chasis and Wildfire, the kids and a pup all owned by Margaret Runnels.

massage. Avoid plastics and any sort of rubber toys, *particularly those with squeakers* which the puppy may remove and swallow. If you want a ball for the puppy to use when playing with him, select one of very hard construction made for this purpose and do not leave it alone with him because he may chew off and swallow bits of the rubber. Take the ball with you when the game is over. This also applies to some of those "tug of war" type rubber toys which are fun when used with the two of you for that purpose but again should *not* be left behind for the dog to work on with his teeth. Bits of swallowed rubber, squeakers, and other such foreign articles can wreak great havoc in the intestinal tract—do all you can to guard against them.

Too many changes all at once can be difficult for a puppy. For at least the first few days he is with you, keep him on the food and feeding schedule to

Barker's Tank of Aramis owned by Linda Barker of Burbank, CA, and Toni and Tim Elitch.

These SBT puppies are by Ch. Reetun's Red Tornado ex Cresstock Game Lady. Age, eight weeks. Owned by Marlene Fund of Mutual Fund Kennels. Photo courtesy of B. Cresse.

which he is accustomed. Find out ahead of time from the breeder what he feeds his puppies, how frequently, and at what times of the day. Also find out what, if any, food supplements the breeder has been using and recommends. Then be prepared by getting in a supply of the same food so that you will have it there when you bring the puppy home. Once the puppy is accustomed to his new surroundings, then you can switch the type of food and schedule to fit your convenience, but for the first several days do it as the puppy expects.

Your selection of a veterinarian should also be attended to before the puppy comes home, because you should stop at the vet's office for the puppy to be checked over as soon as you leave the breeder's premises. If the breeder is from your area, ask him for recommendations. Ask your dog-owning friends for their opinions of the local veterinarians, and see what their experiences with those available have been. Choose someone whom several of your friends recommend highly, then contact him about your puppy, perhaps making an appointment to stop in at his office. If the premises are clean, modern, and well equipped, and if you like the veterinarian, make an appointment to bring the puppy in on the day of purchase. Be sure to obtain the puppy's health record from the

breeder, including information on such things as shots and worming that the puppy has had.

JOINING THE FAMILY

Remember that, exciting and happy an occasion as it is for you, the puppy's move from his place of birth to your home can be, for him, a traumatic experience. His mother and littermates will be missed. He quite likely will be awed or frightened by the change of surroundings. The person on whom he depended will be gone. Everything should be planned to make his arrival at your home pleasant—to give him confidence and to help him realize that yours is a pretty nice place to be after all.　·

Never bring a puppy home on a holiday. There is just too much going on with people and gifts and excitement. If he is in honor of an "occasion," work it out so that his arrival will be a few days earlier, or perhaps even better, a few days later than the "occasion." Then your home will be back to its normal routine and the puppy can enjoy your undivided attention. Try not to bring the puppy home in the evening. Early morning is the ideal time, as then he has the opportunity of getting acquainted and the initial strangeness should wear off before bedtime. You will find it a more peaceful night that way. Allow the puppy to investigate as he likes, under your watchful eye. If you already have a pet in the

household, keep a careful watch that the relationship between the two gets off to a friendly start or you may quickly find yourself with a lasting problem. Much of the future attitude of each toward the other will depend on what takes place that first day, so keep your mind on what they are doing and let your other activities slide for the moment. Be careful not to let your older pet become jealous by paying more attention to the puppy than to him, as that will start a bad

Sooner's Perfectly Demonic, by Ch. Sooner's Our Man Flint ex Sooner's Steamboat Annie. Bred by Olivia Patterson, and owned by John Sparks and Lenna S. Hanna, S'N'S American Staffs.

situation immediately.

If you have a child, here again it is important that the relationship start out well. Before the puppy is brought home, you should have a talk with the youngster. He must clearly understand that puppies are fragile and can easily be injured; therefore, they should not be teased, hurt, mauled, or overly rough-housed. A puppy is not an inanimate toy; it is a

Do not start out by spoiling your puppy. A puppy is usually pretty smart and can be quite demanding. What you had considered to be "just for tonight" may be accepted by the puppy as "for keeps." Be firm with him, strike a routine, and stick to it. The puppy will learn more quickly this way, and everyone will be happier as a result. A radio playing softly or a dim night light are often

A lovely photo of a boy and his dog! Chet Rodgers, III, ex Chet and Lauraine Rodgers of WildWind American Staffordshires of Rhode Island, sitting happily alongside of his pal, Ch. WildWinds Midnight Revenge, C.D., U.D. Young Chet is three here.

living thing with a right to be loved and handled respectfully, treatment which will reflect in the dog's attitude toward your child as both mature together. Never permit your children's playmates to mishandle the puppy, tormenting the puppy until it turns on the children in self-defense. Children often do not realize how rough is too rough. You, as a responsible adult, are obligated to assure that your puppy's relationship with children is a pleasant one.

comforting to a puppy as it gets accustomed to new surroundings and should be provided in preference to bringing the puppy to bed with you—unless, of course, you intend him to share the bed as a permanent arrangement.

SOCIALIZING AND TRAINING

Socialization and training of your puppy should start the very day of his arrival in your home. Never address him without calling him by name. A short, simple name is the easiest to teach as it catches the dog's attention quickly; avoid elaborate call names. Always address the dog by the same name, not a whole series of pet names; the latter will only confuse the puppy.

Use his name clearly, and call the puppy over to you when you see him awake and wandering about. When he comes, make a big fuss over him for being such a good dog. He thus will quickly associate the sound of his name with coming to you and a pleasant happening.

Several hours after the puppy's arrival is not too soon to start accustoming him to the feel of a light collar. He may hardly notice it; or he may struggle, roll over, and try to rub it off his neck with his paws. Divert his attention when this occurs by offering a tasty snack or a toy (starting a game with him) or by petting him. Before long he will have accepted the strange feeling around his neck and no longer appear aware of it. Next comes the lead. Attach it and then immediately take the puppy outside or otherwise try to divert his attention with things to see and sniff. He may struggle against the lead at first, biting at it and trying to free himself. Do not pull him with it at this point; just hold the end loosely and try to follow him if he starts off in any direction. Normally his attention will soon turn to

investigating his surroundings if he is outside or you have taken him into an unfamiliar room in your house; curiosity will take over and he will become interested in sniffing around the surroundings. Follow him with the lead slackly held until he seems to have completely forgotten about it; then try with gentle urging to get him to follow you. Don't be rough or jerk at him; just tug gently on the lead in

Aust. Ch. Almajon Stargazer by Daktari Jarrod—Borstaff Brindy Brillo, is the grandsire of Ch. Pumptail Dragonstar Dancer, U.D., Can. C.D.X.

short quick motions (steady pulling can become a battle of wills), repeating his name or trying to get him to follow your hand which is holding a bite of food or an interesting toy. If you have an older lead-trained dog, then it should be a cinch to get the puppy to follow along after *him*. In any event the average puppy learns quite quickly and will soon be trotting along nicely on the

A huddle well populating Dr. J. Martin's sofa.

"Watch out, that Yorkie's gaining" as a good-natured chase takes place between a tiny Yorkshire Terrier and Am Staff, Ledge Rock's Cherokee Fiddler, who are good friends and spend many hours playing together. Owner, Ruth Prehn.

lead. Once that point has been reached, the next step is to teach him to follow on your left side, or heel. This will not likely be accomplished all in one day; it should be done with short training periods over the course of several days until you are satisfied with the result.

During the course of house training your puppy, you will need to take him out frequently and at regular intervals: first thing in the morning directly from the crate, immediately after meals, after the puppy has

been napping, or when you notice that the puppy is looking for a spot. Choose more or less the same place to take the puppy each time so that a pattern will be established. If he does not go immediately, do not return him to the house as he will probably relieve himself the moment he is inside. Stay out with him until he has finished; then be lavish with your praise for his good behavior. If you catch the puppy having an accident indoors, grab him firmly and rush him outside, sharply saying "No!" as you pick him up. If you do not see the accident occur, there is little point in doing anything except cleaning it up, as once it has happened and been forgotten, the puppy will most likely not even realize why you are scolding him.

If you live in a big city or are away many hours at a time, having a dog that is trained to go on paper has some very definite advantages. To do this, one proceeds pretty much the same way as taking the puppy outdoors, except now you place the puppy on the newspaper at the proper time. The paper should always be kept in the same spot. An easy way to paper train a puppy if you have a playpen for it or an exercise pen is to line the area with newspapers; then gradually, every day or so, remove a section of newspaper until you are down to just one or two. The puppy acquires the habit of using the paper; and as the prepared area grows smaller, in the majority of cases the dog will continue to use whatever paper is still available. It is pleasant, if the dog is alone for an excessive length of time, to be able to feel that if he needs it the paper is there and will be used.

The puppy should form the

expression you use to give a command, stick to the very same one each time for each act. Repetition is the big thing in training—and so is association with what the dog is expected to do. When you mean "Sit," always say exactly that. "Stay" should mean *only* that the dog should remain

Am. and Can. Ch. Evergreen's Demon Seed, C.D., is a Terrier Group winner and a multiple Best of Breed and Group placer.

habit of spending a certain amount of time in his crate, even when you are home. Sometimes the puppy will do this voluntarily, but if not, he should be taught to do so, which is accomplished by leading the puppy over by his collar, gently pushing him inside, and saying firmly, "Down" or "Stay." Whatever

where he receives the command. "Down" means something else again. Do not confuse the dog by shuffling the commands, as this will create training problems for you.

As soon as he had had his immunization shots, take your puppy with you whenever and wherever possible. There is

Ch. Kar-Ron's Gentleman Jim gains Best of Winners at Bronx County, 1985, under judge Ric Chashoudian. Owners, Karen and Ron Tucker of Pennsburg, PA.

BEST OF WINNERS
BRONX COUNTY
KENNEL CLUB
MARCH 1985

nothing that will build a self-confident, stable dog like socialization, and it is extremely important that you plan and give the time and energy necessary for this, whether your dog is to be a show dog or a pleasant, well-adjusted family member. Take your puppy in the car so that he will learn to enjoy riding and not become carsick, as dogs may do if they are infrequent travelers. Take him anywhere you are going where you are certain he will be welcome: visiting friends and relatives (if they do not have housepets who may resent the visit), busy shopping centers (keeping him always on lead), or just walking around the streets of your town. If someone admires him (as always seems to happen when one is out with puppies), encourage the stranger to pet and talk with him. Socialization of this type brings out the best in your puppy and helps him to grow up with a friendly outlook, liking the world and its inhabitants. The worst thing that can be done to a puppy's personality is to shelter him. By always keeping him at home away from things and people unfamiliar to him, you may be creating a personality problem for the mature dog that will be a cross for you to bear later on.

Am Staff puppies politely sharing their bowl. Haus Trevilians Kennels of Doug Loving.

FEEDING YOUR DOG

Time was when providing nourishing food for dogs involved a far more complicated procedure than people now feel is necessary. The old school of thought was that the daily ration must consist of fresh beef, vegetables, cereal, egg yolks, and cottage cheese as basics with such additions as brewer's yeast and vitamin tablets on a daily basis.

During recent years, however, many minds have changed regarding this procedure. Eggs, cottage cheese, and supplements to the diet are still given, but the basic method of feeding dogs has changed; and the change has been, in the opinion of many,

Gorgeous three-week-old puppies, a most excellent and "showy" litter, at S'N'S Kennels, Lenna S. Hanna.

"The school of thought now is that you are doing your dogs a favor when you feed them some of the fine commercially prepared dog foods in preference to your own home-cooked concoctions."

better. The school of thought now is that you are doing your dogs a favor when you feed them some of the fine commercially prepared dog foods in preference to your own home-cooked concoctions.

The reason behind this new outlook is easily understandable. The dog food industry has grown to be a major one, participated in by some of the best known and most respected names in America. These trusted firms, it is agreed, turn out excellent products, so people are feeding their dog food preparations with confidence and the dogs are thriving, living longer, happier, and healthier lives than ever before. What more could one want?

There are at least half a dozen absolutely top-grade dry foods to be mixed with broth or water and served to your dog according to directions. There are all sorts of canned meats, and there are several kinds of "convenience foods," those in a packet which you open and dump out into the dog's dish. It is just that simple. The convenience foods are neat and easy to use when you are away from home, but generally speaking a dry food mixed with hot water (or soup) and meat is preferred. It is the opinion of many that the canned meat, with its added fortifiers, is more beneficial to the dogs than the fresh meat. However, the two can be alternated or, if you prefer and your dog does well on it, by all means use fresh

ground beef. A dog enjoys changes in the meat part of his diet, which is easy with the canned food since all sorts of beef are available (chunk, ground, stewed, and so on), plus lamb, chicken, and even such concoctions as liver and egg, plain liver flavor, and a blend of five meats.

There is also prepared food geared to every age bracket of your dog's life, from puppyhood on through old age, with special additions or modifications to make it particularly nourishing and beneficial. Previous generations never had it so good where the canine dinner is concerned, because these commercially prepared foods are tasty and geared to meeting the dog's gastronomic approval.

Additionally, contents and nutrients are clearly listed on the labels, as are careful instructions for feeding just the right amount for the size, weight, and age of each dog.

With these foods the addition of extra vitamins is not necessary, but if you prefer there are several kinds of those, too, that serve as taste treats as well as being beneficial. Your pet supplier has a full array of them.

Of course there is no reason not to cook up something for your dog if you would feel happier doing so. But it seems unnecessary when such truly satisfactory rations are available with so much less trouble and expense.

How often you feed your dog

is a matter of how it works out best for you. Many owners prefer to do it once a day. It is generally agreed that two meals, each of smaller quantity, are better for the digestion and more satisfying to the dog, particularly if yours is a household member who stands around and watches preparations for the family meals. Do not overfeed. This is the shortest route to all sorts of problems. Follow directions and note carefully how your dog is looking. If your dog is overweight, cut back the quantity of food a bit. If the dog looks thin, then increase the amount. Each dog is an individual and the food intake should be adjusted to his requirements to keep him feeling and looking trim and in top condition.

From the time puppies are fully weaned until they are about twelve weeks old, they should be fed four times daily. From three months to six months of age, three meals should suffice. At six months of

Photo courtesy Lenna S. Hanna, Sword and Sorcery Kennels.

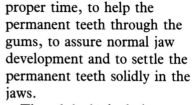

age the puppies can be fed two meals, and the twice daily feedings can be continued until the puppies are close to one year old, at which time feeding can be changed to once daily if desired. If you do feed just once a day, do so by early afternoon at the latest and give the dog a snack, a biscuit or two, at bedtime.

Remember that plenty of fresh water should always be available to your puppy or dog for drinking. This is of utmost importance to his health.

ALL DOGS NEED TO CHEW

Puppies and young dogs need something with resistance to chew on while their teeth and jaws are developing—for cutting the puppy teeth, to induce growth of the permanent teeth under the puppy teeth, to assist in getting rid of the puppy teeth at the

Ch. Cresstock Grand Slam, by Silverlake Hurricane ex Ch. Cresstock Delight, was bred by Bonnie Cresse. This Staffordshire Bull Terrier is owned by Melanie Walker.

proper time, to help the permanent teeth through the gums, to assure normal jaw development and to settle the permanent teeth solidly in the jaws.

The adult dog's desire to chew stems from the instinct for tooth cleaning, gum massage and jaw exercise—plus the need to vent periodic doggie tensions.

Dental caries (decay), as it affects the teeth of humans, is virtually unknown in dogs; but tartar accumulates on the teeth of dogs, particularly at the gum line, more rapidly than on the teeth of humans. These accumulations, if not removed, bring irritation and then infection, which erodes the tooth enamel and ultimately destroys the teeth at the roots. Most chewing by adult dogs is an effort to do something about this problem for themselves.

Tooth and jaw development will normally continue until the dog is more than a year old— but sometimes much longer, depending upon the breed, chewing exercise, the rate at which calcium can be utilized and many other factors, known and unknown, which affect the development of individual dogs. Diseases, like distemper for example, may sometimes arrest development of the teeth and jaws, which may resume months or even years later.

This is why dogs, especially puppies and young dogs, will often destroy property worth hundreds of dollars when their chewing instinct is not diverted

from their owner's possessions, particularly during the widely varying critical period for young dogs. Saving your possessions from destruction, assuring proper development of teeth and jaws, providing for "interim" tooth cleaning and gum massage, and channeling doggie tensions into a non-destructive outlet are, therefore, all dependent upon the dog's having available something suitable when his instinct tells him to chew. If your purposes, and those of your dog, are to be accomplished, what you provide for chewing must be desirable from the doggie viewpoint, have the necessary functional qualities, and, above all, be safe for your dog.

It is very important that dogs

Ch. Ryan's D.J., by Sertoma's Blazing Diamond ex Rush's Little Afton, outstanding winner of Best of Breed and Group placement honors, was bred by Jimmy Ryan and is handled by John McCartney for owner Daniel Scariato, Matamoras, PA.

Ch. Bullseye Double Rank and J. Zane Smith on bended knee.

not be permitted to chew on anything they can break or indigestible things from which they can bite sizeable chunks. Sharp pieces, such as those from a bone which can be broken by a dog, may pierce the intestine wall and kill. Indigestible things which can be bitten off in chunks, such as toys made of rubber compound or cheap plastic, may cause an intestinal stoppage; if not regurgitated, they are certain to bring painful death unless surgery is promptly performed.

Strong natural bones, such as 4 to 8 inch lengths of round shin bone from mature beef—either the kind you can get from your butcher or one of the varieties available commercially in pet stores—may serve your dog's teething needs, if his

mouth is large enough to handle them effectively.

You may be tempted to give your puppy a smaller bone and he may not be able to break it when you do, but puppies grow rapidly and the power of their jaws constantly increases until maturity. This means that a growing dog may break one of the smaller bones at any time, swallow the pieces and die painfully before you realize what is wrong.

Many people have the mistaken notion that their dog's teeth are like those of wild carnivores or of dogs from antiquity. The teeth of wild carnivorous animals and those found in the fossils of the dog-like creatures of antiquity have far thicker and stronger enamel than those of our contemporary dogs.

All hard, natural bones are highly abrasive. If your dog is an avid chewer, natural bones may wear away his teeth prematurely; hence, they then should be taken away from your dog when the teething purposes have been served. The badly worn, and usually painful, teeth of many mature dogs can be traced to excessive chewing on natural bones.

Contrary to popular belief, knuckle bones that can be chewed up and swallowed by the dog provide little, if any, useable calcium or other nutriment. They do, however, disturb the digestion of most dogs and cause them to vomit the nourishing food they need.

Never give a dog your old

shoe to chew on, even if you have removed all the nails or metal parts, such as lace grommets, buckles, metal arches, and so on. Rubber heels are especially dangerous, as the dog can bite off chunks, swallow them, and suffer from intestinal blockage as a result. Additionally, if the rubber should happen to have a nail imbedded in it that you cannot detect, this could pierce or tear the intestinal wall. There is always the possibility, too, that your dog may fail to differentiate between his shoe and yours and chew up a good pair while you're not looking. It is strongly recommended that you refrain from offering old shoes as chew toys since there are much safer products available commercially.

Dried rawhide products have become available during the past few years. They don't serve the primary chewing functions very well, they are a bit messy when wet from mouthing, and most dogs chew them up rather rapidly—but they have been considered safe for dogs until recently. Now, more and more incidents of death, and near death, by strangulation have been reported to be the result of partially swallowed chunks of rawhide swelling in the throat. Currently, some veterinarians have been attributing cases of acute constipation to large pieces of incompletely digested rawhide in the intestine.

The nylon bones, especially those with natural meat and

bone fractions added, are probably the most complete, safe and economical answer to the chewing need. Dogs cannot break them or bite off sizeable chunks; hence, they are completely safe. And being longer lasting than other things offered for the purpose, they are economical.

Hard chewing raises little bristle-like projections on the surface of the nylon bones to provide effective interim tooth

Proven safe and effective, nylon chew products are available at local pet shops everywhere.

Missy Yuhl captures Cock 'N' Bull's Ch. Oltyme's Cock O' The Walk placing Best of Breed with handler Jerry E. Brown.

Ch. Fraja's E.C. Dodge City, gray brindle and white, weighs 67 pounds and stands 20.5 inches high. This handsome dog was No. 3 Staff in the country, 1984, and is especially admired for his movement. Owners, Bill Olin and Jon King. Handler, John McCartney.

cleaning and vigorous gum massage, much in the same way your tooth brush does for you. The little projections are raked off and swallowed in the form of thin shavings, but the chemistry of the nylon is such that they break down in the stomach fluids and pass through without effect.

The toughness of the nylon provides the strong chewing resistance needed for important jaw exercise and effective help for the teething functions; however, there is no tooth wear because nylon is non-abrasive. Being inert, nylon does not support the growth of microorganisms; and it can be washed in soap and water, or it can be sterilized by boiling or in an autoclave.

There are a great variety of Nylabone® products available that veterinarians recommend as safe and healthy for your dog or puppy to chew on. These nylon pooch pacifiers—Nylabone®, Nylaball®—can't splinter, chip, or break off in large chunks; instead, they are frizzled by the dog's chewing action, and this creates a toothbrush-like surface that cleanses the teeth and massages the gums. At the same time, these hard-nylon therapeutic devices channel doggie tension and chewing frustation into constructive rather than destructive behavior. Check your local pet shop for the *only* chew products made of flavor-impregnated solid nylon; and be sure to ask about the various sizes, shapes, and flavors that are manufactured for your dog's needs. If you want a soft, chewy play toy, look for Gumabone® wherever Nylabone® products are sold. These flexible nylon bones are designed to provide entertainment for you and your dog, and they are great aids for teaching your canine companion how to retrieve.

Nothing, however, substitutes for periodic professional attention to your dog's teeth and gums, not any more than your toothbrush can do that for you. Have your dog's teeth cleaned by your veterinarian at least once a year—twice a year is better—and he will be healthier, happier and a far more pleasant companion.

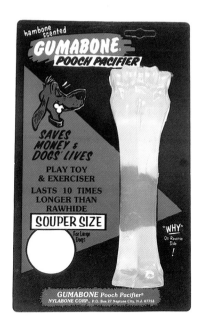

The Nylabone® and Gumabone® product lines represent the original nylon and polyeurothane chew devices. Clinical studies have proven that regular use of the Gumabone® will reduce plaque accumulation substantially.

The Making of a Show Dog

If you have decided to become a show dog exhibitor, you have accepted a very real and very exciting challenge. The groundwork has been accomplished with the selection of your future show prospect. If you have purchased a puppy, it is assumed that you have gone through all the proper preliminaries concerning good care, which should be the same if the puppy is a pet or future show dog, with a few added precautions for the latter.

GENERAL CONSIDERATIONS

Remember the importance of keeping your future winner in trim, top condition. Since you want him neither too fat nor too thin, his appetite for his proper diet should be guarded, and children and guests should not be permitted to constantly feed him "goodies." The best treat of all is a small wad of raw ground beef or a packaged dog treat. To be avoided are ice cream, cake, cookies, potato chips, and other fattening items which will cause the dog to put on weight and may additionally spoil his appetite for the proper, nourishing, well-balanced diet so essential to good health and condition.

The importance of temperament and showmanship cannot possibly be overestimated. They have put many a mediocre dog across, while lack of them can ruin the career of an otherwise outstanding specimen. From the day your dog joins your family, socialize him. Keep him accustomed to being with people and to being handled by people. Encourage your friends and relatives to "go over" him as the judges will in the ring so this will not seem a strange and upsetting experience. Practice showing his "bite" (the manner in which his teeth meet) quickly and deftly. It is quite simple to slip the lips apart with your fingers, and the puppy should be willing to accept this from you or the

Opposite: Ch. S'N'S Ogre Easy, Am Staff owned by D.K. Loving, Haus Trevilians, and Lenna S. Hanna.

Mr. and Mrs. Alex Mudie's Casey placing fourth under judge Ed Bevin at the Kawartha Dog Show. Steve Selwood, handler.

judge without struggle.

Some judges prefer that the exhibitors display the dog's bite and other mouth features themselves. These are the considerate ones, who do not wish to chance the spreading of possible infection from dog to dog with their hands on each one's mouth—a courtesy particularly appreciated in these days of virus epidemics. But the old-fashioned judges still persist in doing it themselves, so the dog should be ready for either possibility.

Take your future show dog with you in the car, thus accustoming him to riding so that he will not become carsick on the day of a dog show. He should associate pleasure and attention with going in the car, van, or motor home. Take him where it is crowded: downtown, to the shops, everywhere you go that dogs are permitted. Make the expeditions fun for him by frequent petting and words of praise; do not just ignore him as you go about your errands.

Do not overly shelter your future show dog. Instinctively you may want to keep him at home where he is safe from germs or danger. This can be foolish on two counts. The first reason is that a puppy kept away from other dogs builds up no natural immunity against all the things with which he will come in contact at dog shows, so it is wiser to keep him up-to-date on all protective shots and then let him become accustomed to being among dogs and dog owners. Also, a dog who is never among strange people, in strange places, or among strange dogs may grow up with a shyness or timidity of spirit that will cause you real problems as his show career draws near.

Keep your show prospect's coat in immaculate condition with frequent grooming and daily brushing. When bathing is necessary, use a mild dog shampoo or whatever the breeder of your puppy may suggest. Several of the brand-name products do an excellent job. Be sure to rinse thoroughly so as not to risk skin irritation by traces of soap left behind, and protect against soap entering the eyes by a drop of castor oil in each before you lather up. Use warm water (be sure it is not uncomfortably hot or chillingly cold) and a good spray. Make certain you allow your dog to dry thoroughly in a warm, draft-free area (or outdoors, if it is warm and sunny) so that he doesn't catch cold. Then proceed to groom him to perfection.

A show dog's teeth must be kept clean and free of tartar. Nylon bones or hard dog biscuits can help, but if tartar accumulates, see that it is removed promptly by your veterinarian. Bones for chewing are not suitable for show dogs as they tend to damage and wear down the tooth enamel.

Assuming that you will be handling the dog yourself, or even if he will be professionally handled, a few moments each day of dog show routine is important. Practice setting him up as you have seen the exhibitors do at the shows you've attended, and teach him to hold this position once you have him stacked to your satisfaction. Make the learning period pleasant by being firm but lavish in your praise when he responds correctly. Teach him to gait at your side at a moderate rate on a loose lead. When you have mastered the basic essentials at home, then hunt out and join a training class for future work. Training classes are sponsored by show-giving clubs in many areas, and their popularity is steadily increasing. If you have no other way of locating one, perhaps your veterinarian would know

Noted winner Ch. Ledge Rock's Kopper Korn has gained such show honors as winning the Sweepstakes at the National Specialty in 1984, taking Best of Winners in the regular classes at the Specialty as well as at the AKC Centennial Dog Show. Pictured here at 12 months.

159

of one through some of his other clients; but if you are sufficiently aware of the dog show world to want a show dog, you will probably be personally acquainted with other people who will share information of this type with you.

Accustom your show dog to being in a crate (which you should be doing with a pet dog as well). He should relax in his crate at the shows "between times" for his own well being and safety.

MATCH SHOWS

Your show dog's initial experience in the ring should be in match show competition. This type of event is intended as a learning experience for both the dog and the exhibitor. You will not feel embarrassed or out of place no matter how poorly your puppy may behave or how inept your attempts at handling may be, as you will find others there with the same type of problems. The important thing is that you get the puppy out and into a show

Ch. Bullseye Forget-Me-Not at Scottsdale K.C. in 1980. Bred, owned and handled by J. Zane Smith. A daughter of Ch. Reetun's Lord Jim ex Ch. Piltdown Miss Equal, Forget-Me Not is the dam of Ch. Bullseye Double Rank.

Ch. Cresstock Logo of Linden at one year, sired by Linden Spike of Taurus, his dam was Ch. Cresstock Delight. Bred by Bonnie Cresse, Logo is owned by Jack Crowther.

ring where the two of you can practice together and learn the ropes.

Only on rare occasions is it necessary to make match show entries in advance, and even those with a pre-entry policy will usually accept entries at the door as well. Thus you need not plan several weeks ahead, as is the case with point shows, but can go when the mood strikes you. Also there is a vast difference in the cost, as match show entries only cost a few dollars while entry fees for the point shows may be over ten dollars, an amount none of us needs to waste until we have some idea of how the puppy will behave or how much more pre-show training is needed.

Match shows are frequently judged by professional handlers who, in addition to making the awards, are happy to help new exhibitors with comments and advice on their puppies and their presentation of them. Avail yourself of all these opportunities before heading out to the sophisticated world of the point shows.

POINT SHOWS

As previously mentioned, entries for American Kennel Club point shows must be made in advance. This must be done on an official entry blank of the show-giving club. The entry

Left: **Ch. Ledge Rock's Ruckey Velvet at age six months. Bred and owned by Ernest and Ruth Prehn. *Right:* Coalminer I'm A Blueberry Too, a future champion. Owner, Robert W. Calladine of Ontario, Canada. This well-balanced bitch is a daughter of British import, Topcroft Minstrel ex Peck's Sexy Pants from USA. Blue in color, she was bred by Evelyn Frei.**

must then be filed either personally or by mail with the show superintendent or the show secretary (if the event is being run by the club members alone and a superintendent has not been hired, this information will appear on the premium list) in time to reach its destination prior to the published closing date or filling of the quota. These entries must be made carefully, must be signed by the owner of the dog or the owner's agent (your professional handler), and must

specific show. If a registered dog has been acquired by a new owner, it must be entered in the name of the new owner in any show for which entries close after the date of acquirement, regardless of whether the new owner has or has not actually received the registration certificate indicating that the dog is recorded in his name. State on the entry form whether or not transfer application has been mailed to the American Kennel Club, and it goes without

be accompanied by the entry fee; otherwise they will not be accepted. Remember that it is not when the entry leaves your hands that counts, but the date of arrival at its destination. If you are relying on the mails, which are not always dependable, get the entry off well before the deadline to avoid disappointment.

A dog must be entered at a dog show in the name of the actual owner at the time of the entry closing date of that

saying that the latter should be attended to promptly when you purchase a registered dog.

In filling out your entry blank, type, print, or write clearly, paying particular attention to the spelling of names, correct registration numbers, and so on. Also, if there is more than one variety in your breed, be sure to indicate into which category your dog is being entered.

The **Puppy Class** is for dogs or bitches who are six months of age and under twelve months and who are not champions. The age of a dog shall be calculated up to and inclusive of the first day of a show. For example, the first day a dog whelped on January 1st is eligible to compete in a Puppy Class at a show is July 1st of the same year; and he may continue to compete in Puppy Classes up to and including a show on December 31 of the same year, but he is *not* eligible to compete in a Puppy Class at a show held on or after January 1 of the following year.

The Puppy Class is the first one in which you should enter your puppy. In it a certain allowance will be made for the fact that they *are* puppies, thus an immature dog or one displaying less than perfect showmanship will be less severely penalized than, for instance, would be the case in Open. It is also quite likely that others in the class will be suffering from these problems, too. When you enter a puppy, be sure to check the

Ch. Athenian Angel is known to owner Joe LeBlanc as "Pookie."

Ch. Ledge Rock's Kopper Korn placing in the Group for owners Ernest and Ruth Prehn.

classification with care, as some shows divide their Puppy Class into a 6-9 months old section and a 9-12 months old section.

The **Novice Class** is for dogs six months of age and over, whelped in the United States or Canada, who *prior to the official closing date for entries* have *not* won three first prizes in the Novice Class, any first prize at all in the Bred-by-Exhibitor, American-bred, or Open Classes, or one or more points toward championship. The provisions for this class are confusing to many people, which is probably the reason exhibitors do not enter in it more frequently. A dog may win any number of first prizes in the Puppy Class and still retain his eligibility for Novice. He may place second, third, or fourth not only in Novice on an unlimited number of occasions, but also in Bred-by-Exhibitor, American-bred and Open and still remain eligible for Novice. But he may no longer be shown in Novice when he has won three blue ribbons in that class, when he has won even one blue ribbon in either Bred-by-Exhibitor, American-bred, or Open, or when he has won a single championship point.

In determining whether or not a dog is eligible for the Novice Class, keep in mind the fact that previous wins are calculated according to the official published date for closing of entries, not by the date on which you may actually have made the entry. So if in the interim, between the time you made the entry and the official closing date, your dog makes a win causing him to become ineligible for Novice, change your class *immediately* to another for which he will be eligible, preferably either Bred-by-Exhibitor or American-bred. To do this, you must contact the show's superintendent or secretary, at first by telephone to save time and then in writing to confirm it. The Novice Class always seems to have the fewest entries of any class, and therefore it is a splendid "practice ground" for you and your young dog while you are getting the "feel" of being in the ring.

Bred-by-Exhibitor Class is for dogs whelped in the United States or, if individually registered in the American Kennel Club Stud Book, for dogs whelped in Canada who are six months of age or older, are not champions, and are owned wholly or in part by the person or by the spouse of the person who was the breeder or one of the breeders of record. Dogs entered in this class must be handled in the class by an owner or by a member of the immediate family of the owner. Members of an immediate family for this purpose are husband, wife, father, mother, son, daughter, brother, or sister. This is the class which is really the "breeders' showcase," and the one which breeders should enter with particular pride to show off their achievements.

The **American-bred Class** is for all dogs excepting champions, six months of age or older, who were whelped in the United States by reason of a mating which took place in the United States.

The **Open Class** is for any dog six months of age or older (this is the only restriction for this class). Dogs with championship points compete in it, dogs who are already champions are eligible to do so, dogs who are imported can be entered, and, of course, American-bred dogs compete in it. This class is, for some strange reason, the favorite of exhibitors who are "out to win." They rush to enter their

Ch. Charbert's Diamond Jim winning Best of Opposite under the author at the Windham County K. C. in 1985.

Top: Ch. Call Me Katie Scarlet, by Ch. Tara's Doc Holliday ex Ch. Tara's Muddi Fields Forever, finishing here at age 12 months. Bred by Kaye N. Roberts. Owned by Mrs. Hugh C. Brown, Jr. *Bottom:* Ch. Ledge Rock's Kopper Korn, by Ch. Titan's Rojo Grande ex Ch. Rowdytown Jazz of Ledge Rock, is a homebred owned by Ernest and Ruth Prehn.

Top: Dagmar, owned by John C. McCartney, is shown here winning Best of Breed for the second straight year at Westminster, 1982.
Bottom: Ch. Ryan's Hot Stuff taking Best of Breed, Am Staff, at Windham County K.C., November, 1985, with handler Bonnie Sellner.

pointed dogs in it, under the false impression that by doing so they assure themselves of greater attention from the judges. This really is not so, and some people feel that to enter in one of the less competitive classes, with a better chance of winning it and thus earning a second opportunity of gaining the

The kind of head we love to see in Am Staffs. This is Rambo, whose dam is the illustrious "Dagmar." Photo courtesy of John C. McCartney.

judge's approval by returning to the ring in the Winners Class, can often be a more effective strategy.

One does not enter the **Winners Class.** One earns the right to compete in it by winning first prize in Puppy, Novice, Bred-by-Exhibitor, American-bred, or Open. No dog who has been defeated on the same day in one of these classes is eligible to compete for Winners, and every dog who has been a blue-ribbon winner in one of them and not defeated in another, should he have been entered in more than one class (as occasionally happens), *must* do so. Following the selection of the Winners Dog or the Winners Bitch, the dog or bitch receiving that award leaves the ring. Then the dog or bitch who placed second in that class, unless previously beaten by another dog or bitch in another class at the same show, re-enters the ring to compete against the remaining first-prize winners for Reserve. The latter award indicates that the dog or bitch selected for it is standing "in reserve" should the one who received Winners be disqualified or declared ineligible through any technicality when the awards are checked at the American Kennel Club. In that case, the one who placed Reserve is moved up to Winners, at the same time receiving the appropriate championship points.

Winners Dog and Winners Bitch are the awards which

carry points toward championship with them. The points are based on the number of dogs or bitches actually in

bring the total to fifteen. When your dog has gained fifteen points as described above, a championship certificate will be

WINNERS

DEVON DOG SHOW
ASSOCIATION INC

KLEIN   OCT 1981

At six months of age, Ch. Kirkees Polar Bear of Fraja was Winners Bitch from the Puppy Classes at Hatboro, Devon and Montgomery. She later won at the National Specialty. Owned by W.M. Chariff and Jon King.

competition, and the points are scaled one through five, the latter being the greatest number available to any one dog or bitch at any one show. Three-, four-, or five-point wins are considered majors. In order to become a champion, a dog or bitch must have won two majors under two different judges, plus at least one point from a third judge, and the additional points necessary to

issued to you, and your dog's name will be published in the champions of record list in the *Pure-Bred Dogs/American Kennel Gazette*, the official publication of the American Kennel Club.

The scale of championship points for each breed is worked out by the American Kennel Club and reviewed annually, at which time the number required in competition may be either changed (raised or

Ch. Cresstock Logo of Linden at one year. By Linden Spike of Taurus ex Ch. Cresstock Delight. Bred by Bonnie Cresse and owned by Jack Crowther. A Best of Breed winner.

BEST OF WINNERS
MID CONTINENT KENNEL CLUB
1985
PHOTO BY PETRULIS

lowered) or remain the same. The scale of championship points for all breeds is published annually in the May issue of the *Gazette*, and the current ratings for each breed within that area are published in every show catalog.

When a dog or bitch is adjudged Best of Winners, its championship points are, for that show, compiled on the basis of which sex had the greater number of points. If there are two points in dogs and four in bitches and the dog goes Best of Winners, then *both* the dog and the bitch are awarded an equal number of points, in this case four. Should the Winners Dog or the Winners Bitch go on to win Best of Breed or Best of Variety, additional points are accorded for the additional dogs and bitches defeated by so doing, provided, of course, that there were entries specifically for Best of Breed competition or Specials, as these specific entries are generally called.

If your dog or bitch takes Best of Opposite Sex after going Winners, points are credited according to the number of the same sex defeated in both the regular classes and Specials competition. If Best of Winners is also won, then whatever additional points for each of these awards are available will be credited. Many a one- or two-point win has grown into a major in this manner.

Moving further along, should your dog win its **Variety Group** from the classes (in other words, if it has taken either Winners Dog or Winners Bitch), you then receive points based on the greatest number of points awarded to any member of any breed included within that Group during that show's competition. Should the day's winning also include Best in Show, the same rule of thumb applies, and your dog or bitch receives the highest number of points awarded to any other dog of any breed at that event.

A tribute to the Fraja American Staffordshires: all three of these 1981 Westminster winners are from Fraja bloodlines. Jacqueline Fraser, owner of the Fraja Kennels, is on the far right of this photo. The Best of Breed, first Staff on the left, is "Dagmar" with her owner-handler John McCartney. The judge is Mrs. Barbara Keenan.

Best of Breed competition consists of the Winners Dog and the Winners Bitch, who automatically compete on the strength of those awards, in addition to whatever dogs and bitches have been entered specifically for this class for which champions of record are eligible. Since July 1980, dogs who, according to their owner's records, have completed the requirements for a championship after the closing of entries for the show (but whose championships are unconfirmed) may be transferred from one of the regular classes to the Best of Breed competition, provided this transfer is made by the show superintendent or show secretary *prior to the start of any judging at the show*.

This has proved an extremely popular new rule, as under it a dog can finish on Saturday and then be transferred and compete as a Special on Sunday. It must be emphasized that *the change must be made prior to the start of any part of the day's judging, not for just your individual breed.*

In the United States, Best of Breed winners are entitled to compete in the Variety Group which includes them. This is not mandatory; it is a privilege which exhibitors value. (In Canada, Best of Breed winners *must* compete in the Variety Group or they lose any points already won.) The dogs winning *first* in each of the seven Variety Groups *must* compete for Best in Show. Missing the opportunity of taking your dog in for competition in its Group is foolish, as it is there where the general public is most likely to notice your breed and become interested in learning about it.

Non-regular classes are sometimes included at the all-

Top: Ch. Sooner's Dr. Pepper, an Am Staff owned by Elmer Parsons. Photo by Don Petrulis Photography. *Bottom:* Ch. Steeltown's Blue Monday, the well-known Terrier-Group-winning Am Staff from Cock 'N' Bull Kennels. Handled here by Mike Shea to one of his many victories for owners Dr. Jerry E. and Julianna A. Brown.

"When your dog wins its Variety Group from the Classes, it then receives points based on the greatest number of points awarded to any other member of the Group during the competition of that day."

Ch. S'N'S Ogre Easy is Group-placing for owner Doug Loving under judge Marcia Foy at Riverhead K.C.

breed shows, and they are almost invariably included at Specialty shows. These include Stud Dog Class and Brood Bitch Class, which are judged on the basis of the quality of the two offspring accompanying the sire or dam. The quality of the latter is beside the point and should not be considered by the judge; it is the youngsters who count, and the quality of *both* are to be

Am. and Can. Ch. Steinstaff Goin' For The Gusto, Am. and Can. C.D., winning a Terrier Group placement at Kalamazoo, MI, in May, 1986. At age two-and-a-half years, this fine young SBT belongs to Ellis and Faith Steinman.

TERRIER GROUP

averaged to decide which sire or dam is the best and most consistent producer. Then there is the Brace Class (which, at all-breed shows, moves up to Best Brace in each Variety Group and then Best Brace in Show) which is judged on the similarity and evenness of appearance of the two brace members. In other words, the two dogs should look like identical twins in size, color, and conformation and should move together almost as a single dog, one person handling with precision and ease. The same applies to the Team Class competition, except that four dogs are involved and, if necessary, two handlers.

The Veterans Class is for the older dog, the minimum age of whom is seven years. This class is judged on the quality of the dogs, as the winner competes in Best of Breed competition and has, on a respectable number of occasions, been known to take that top award. So the point is *not* to pick out the oldest dog, as some judges seem to believe, but the best specimen of the breed, exactly as in the regular classes.

Then there are Sweepstakes and Futurity Stakes sponsored by many Specialty clubs, sometimes as part of their regular Specialty shows and sometimes as separate events on an entirely different occasion. The difference between the two stakes is that Sweepstakes entries usually include dogs from six to eighteen months of age with entries made at the same time as the others for the show, while for a Futurity the entries are bitches nominated when bred and the individual puppies entered at or shortly following their birth.

JUNIOR SHOWMANSHIP COMPETITION

If there is a youngster in your family between the ages of ten and sixteen, there is no better or more rewarding hobby than becoming an active participant

Ch. Evergreen's Earth Angel, who with her dam, Ch. Evergreen's Sundancer, makes up her owner's famed Best in Show Winning Brace. Angel is sired by Ch. Tryarr Diamondback Redbolt. Bred and owned by Jim and Carolyn Brown, Evergreen Staffs.

in Junior Showmanship. This is a marvelous activity for young people. It teaches responsibility, good sportsmanship, the fun of competition where one's own skills are the deciding factor of success, proper care of a pet, and how to socialize with other young folks. Any youngster may experience the thrill of emerging from the ring a winner and the satisfaction of a good job well done.

Entry in Junior Showmanship Classes is open to any boy or girl who is at least ten years old and under seventeen years old on the day of the show. The Novice Junior Showmanship Class is open to youngsters who have not already won, at the time the entries close, three firsts in this class. Youngsters who have won three firsts in Novice may compete in the Open Junior Showmanship Class. Any junior handler who wins his third first-place award in Novice may participate in the Open Class at the same show, provided that the Open Class has at least one other junior handler entered and competing in it that day. The Novice and Open Classes may be divided into Junior and Senior Classes. Youngsters between the ages of ten and twelve, inclusively, are eligible for the Junior division; and youngsters between thirteen and seventeen, inclusively, are eligible for the Senior division.

Any of the foregoing classes may be separated into individual classes for boys and for girls. If such a division is made, it must be so indicated on the premium list. The premium list also indicates the prize for Best Junior Handler, if such a prize is being offered at the show. Any youngster who wins a first in any of the regular classes may enter the

The awarding of championship points is based on the total number of dogs in a given competition.

Int. Ch. Herrings Beau Jangles is owned by Chet and Lauraine Rodgers.

BEST OF
BREED OR VARIETY

MARYLAND
KENNEL CLUB
1987   KERNAN

Ch. True Grit Cisco of Sligo, sired by Ch. True Grit Sureshot Magnum ex True Grit Two Tonetess. Breeder, Randal J. Perry. Owners, D.K. Loving and Haus Trevilians.

competition for this prize, provided the youngster has been undefeated in any other Junior Showmanship Class at that show.

Junior Showmanship Classes, unlike regular conformation classes in which the quality of the dog is judged, are judged solely on the skill and ability of the junior handling the dog. Which dog is best is not the point—it is which youngster does the best job with the dog that is under consideration. Eligibility requirements for the dog being shown in Junior Showmanship, and other detailed information, can be found in *Regulations for Junior Showmanship*, available from the American Kennel Club.

A junior who has a dog that

he or she can enter in both Junior Showmanship and conformation classes has twice the opportunity for success and twice the opportunity to get into the ring and work with the dog, a combination which can lead to not only awards for expert handling, but also, if the dog is of sufficient quality, for making a conformation champion.

PRE-SHOW PREPARATIONS

Preparation of the items you will need as a dog show exhibitor should not be left until the last moment. They should be planned and arranged several days in advance of the show in order for you to remain calm and relaxed as the countdown starts.

The importance of the crate has already been mentioned and should already be part of your equipment. Of equal importance is the grooming table, which very likely you have also already acquired for use at home. You should take it along with you to the shows, as your dog will need last minute touches before entering the ring. Should you have not yet made this purchase, folding tables with rubber tops are made specifically for this purpose and can be purchased at most dog shows, where concession booths with marvelous assortments of "doggy" necessities are to be found, or at your pet supplier. You will also need a sturdy tack box (also available at the dog show concessions) in which to carry your grooming tools and equipment. The latter should

include: brushes; combs; scissors; nail clippers; whatever you use for last minute clean-up jobs; cotton swabs; first-aid equipment; and anything you are in the habit of using on the dog, including a leash or two of the type you prefer, some well-cooked and dried-out liver or any of the small packaged "dog treats" for use as bait in the ring, an atomizer in case you wish to dampen your dog's coat when you are preparing him for the ring, and so on. A large turkish towel to spread under the dog on the grooming table is also useful.

Take a large thermos or cooler of ice, the biggest one you can accommodate in your vehicle, for use by "man and beast." Take a jug of water (there are lightweight, inexpensive ones available at all sporting goods shops) and a water dish. If you plan to feed

Ch. Ledge Rock's Lucy In The Sky, an Am Staff owned by Joye Lucarelli and Ruth Prehn. Photo by Martin Booth.

Ch. Lochness Ravoon Buster, by Ch. Doc's Little Grundoon ex Ch. Davenhill's Silverlake Raven, was born in February, 1979. She is a double granddaughter of the good English import Bringarry Dangerman, and her sire Grundoon was a litter brother of Ch. Doc's Little Irate Irene. Bred by Tom and Shelley Lochner, Buster here is making a first major win from the Puppy Class. The handler is Paul R. Hunt.

the dog at the show, or if you and the dog will be away from home more than one day, bring food for him from home so that he will have the type to which he is accustomed.

You may or may not have an exercise pen. While the shows do provide areas for exercise of the dogs, these are among the most likely places to have your dog come in contact with any illnesses which may be going around, and having a pen of your own for your dog's use is excellent protection. Such a pen comes in handy while you're travelling; since it is roomier than a crate, it becomes a comfortable place for your dog to relax and move around in, especially when you're at motels or rest stops. These pens are available at the show concession stands and come in a variety of heights and sizes. A set of "pooper scoopers" should also be part of your equipment, along with a package of plastic

bags for cleaning up after your dog.

Bring along folding chairs for the members of your party, unless all of you are fond of standing, as these are almost never provided by the clubs. Have your name stamped on the chairs so that there will be no doubt as to whom the chairs belong. Bring whatever you and your family enjoy for drinks or snacks in a picnic basket or cooler, as show food, in general, is expensive and usually not great. You should always have a pair of boots, a raincoat, and a rain hat with you (they should remain permanently in your vehicle if you plan to attend shows regularly), as well as a sweater, a warm coat, and a change of shoes. A smock or big cover-up apron will assure that you remain tidy as you prepare the dog for the ring. Your overnight case should include a small sewing kit for emergency

Leoline Gallant Hussar, handled by J. David Massey, here is winning Best of Breed under noted authority Dr. John H. Martin at Berrien Springs, MI, June, 1982.

BEST OF
BREED
OR VARIETY
BOOTH PHOTO

repairs, bandaids, headache and indigestion remedies, and any personal products or medications you normally use.

In your car, you should always carry maps of the area where you are headed and an assortment of motel directories. Generally speaking, Holiday Inns have been found to be the nicest about taking dogs. Ramadas and Howard Johnsons generally do so cheerfully (with a few exceptions). Best Western generally frowns on pets (not always, but often enough to make it necessary to find out which do). Some of the smaller chains welcome pets; the majority of privately-owned motels do not.

Have everything prepared the night before the show to expedite your departure. Be sure that the dog's identification and your judging program and other show information are in your purse or briefcase. If you are taking sandwiches, have them ready. Anything that goes into the car the night before the show will be one thing less to remember in the morning. Decide upon what you will wear and have it out and ready. If there is any question in your mind about what to wear, try on the possibilities before the day of the show; don't risk feeling you may want to change when you see yourself dressed a few moments prior to departure time!

In planning your outfit, make it something simple that

Ch. Tara's Muddi Fields Forever, by Ch. Sindelar's Doctor Mudd ex Ch. Fryarr Strawberry Fields, was bred by Leroy and Lucille Walters; she is owned by Kaye N. Roberts and Stacie Lee Brown.

VARIETY GROUP
THIRD
FORSYTH
KENNEL CLUB
DECEMBER 1985
PHOTO BY BONNIE

will not detract from your dog. Remember that a dark dog silhouettes attractively against a light background and vice-versa. Sport clothes always seem to look best at dog shows, preferably conservative in type and not overly "loud" as you do not want to detract from your dog, who should be the focus of interest at this point. What you wear on your feet is important. Many types of flooring can be hazardously slippery, as can wet grass.

Make it a habit to wear rubber soles and low or flat heels in the ring for your own safety, especially if you are showing a dog that likes to move out smartly.

Your final step in pre-show preparation is to leave yourself plenty of time to reach the show that morning. Traffic can get amazingly heavy as one nears the immediate area of the show, finding a parking place can be difficult, and other delays may occur. You'll be in better humor to enjoy the day if your trip to the show is not fraught with panic over fear of not arriving in time!

ENJOYING THE DOG SHOW

From the moment of your arrival at the show until after your dog has been judged, keep foremost in your mind the fact that he is your reason for being there and that he should therefore be the center of your attention. Arrive early enough to have time for those last-minute touches that can make a great difference when he enters the ring. Be sure that he has ample time to exercise and that he attends to personal matters. A dog arriving in the ring and immediately using it as an exercise pen hardly makes a favorable impression on the judge.

When you reach ringside, ask the steward for your arm-card and anchor it firmly into place on your arm. Make sure that you are where you should be when your class is called. The fact that you have picked up your arm-card does not guarantee, as some seem to think, that the judge will wait for you. The judge has a full schedule which he wishes to complete on time. Even though you may be nervous, assume an air of calm self-confidence. Remember that this is a hobby to be enjoyed, so approach it in that state of mind. The dog will do better, too, as he will be quick to reflect your attitude.

Can. Ch. Coalminer's Boy Minstrel, by Ch. Topcroft Minstrel ex Ch. Peck's Sexy Pants, finishing his title at 16 months of age by going Best of Breed over "Specials." Handled by Tracy Dineley, owned by Alex Mudie, and bred by Evelyn Frei.

Ch. Val Verde
Hesione and
Val Verde
Gentry.
These two
outstanding
SBTs are
owned by Kay
A. Benoit,
Woodlinville,
WA.

Always show your dog with an air of pride. If you make mistakes in presenting him, don't worry about it. Next time you will do better. Do not permit the presence of more experienced exhibitors to intimidate you. After all, they, too, were once newcomers.

The judging routine usually starts when the judge asks that the dogs be gaited in a circle around the ring. During this period the judge is watching each dog as it moves, noting style, topline, reach and drive, head and tail carriage, and general balance. Keep your mind and your eye on your dog, moving him at his most becoming gait and keeping your place in line without coming too close to the exhibitor ahead of you. Always keep your dog on the inside of the circle, between yourself and the judge, so that the judge's view of the dog is unobstructed.

Calmly pose the dog when requested to set up for examination. If you are at the head of the line and many dogs are in the class, go all the way to the end of the ring before starting to stack the dog, leaving sufficient space for those behind you to line theirs up as well, as requested by the judge. If you are not at the head of the line but between other exhibitors, leave sufficient space ahead of your dog for the judge to examine him. The dogs should be spaced so that the judge is able to move among them to see them from all angles. In practicing to "set up" or "stack" your dog for the judge's examination, bear in mind the importance of doing so quickly and with dexterity. The judge has a schedule to meet and only a few moments in which to evaluate each dog. You will immeasurably help yours to make a favorable impression if you are able to "get it all together" in a minimum amount of time. Practice at home before a mirror can be a great help toward bringing this about, facing the dog so that you see him from the same side that the judge will and working to make him look right in the shortest length of time.

Listen carefully as the judge describes the manner in which the dog is to be gaited, whether it is straight down and straight back; down the ring, across, and back; or in a triangle. The latter has become the most popular pattern with the majority of judges. "In a triangle" means the dog should

Ch. Normandie Ides of March completing her title with this win at Bronx County K.C. in April, 1983, under the author. This homebred is owned by Jeanne Pierrette Dross, Albany, NY, and is handled here by Diane Correia. Normandie is a daughter of Ch. Piltdown Keltic Druid ex Ch. Normandie Lady of Shars.

move down the outer side of the ring to the first corner, across that end of the ring to the second corner, and then back to the judge from the second corner, using the center of the ring in a diagonal line. Please learn to do this pattern without breaking at each corner which you move your dog is tremendously important and considerable study and thought should be given to the matter. At home, have someone move the dog for you at different speeds so that you can tell which shows him off to best advantage. The most becoming

Second place, third leg on C.D., September, 1981: Ch. Pumptail Dragonstar Dancer, U.D., Can. C.D.X., with owner-trainer-handler, Faith Steinman, Michigan City, IN.

to twirl the dog around you, a senseless maneuver that has been noticed on occasion. Judges like to see the dog in an uninterrupted triangle, as they are thus able to get a better idea of the dog's gait.

It is impossible to overemphasize that the gait at action almost invariably is seen at a moderate gait, head up and topline holding. Do not gallop your dog around the ring or hurry him into a speed atypical of his breed. Nothing being rushed appears at its best; give your dog a chance to move along at his (and the breed's)

Ch. Kar-Ron's Finwar's Solace, owned by Karen and Ron Tucker, Kar-Ron Kennels, Pennsburg, PA, winning Best of Breed at Harrisburg K.C. in 1985.

natural gait. For a dog's action to be judged accurately, that dog should move with strength and power, but not excessive speed, holding a straight line as he goes to and from the judge.

As you bring the dog back to the judge, stop him a few feet away and be sure that he is standing in a becoming position. Bait him to show the judge an alert expression, using whatever tasty morsel he has been trained to expect for this purpose or, if that works better for you, use a small squeak-toy in your hand. A reminder, please, to those using liver or treats: take them with you when you leave the ring. Do

not just drop them on the ground where they will be found by another dog.

When the awards have been made, accept yours graciously, no matter how you actually may feel about it. What's done is done, and arguing with a judge or stomping out of the ring is useless and a reflection on your sportsmanship. Be courteous, congratulate the winner if your dog was defeated, and try not to show your disappointment. By the same token, please be a gracious winner; this, surprisingly, sometimes seems to be still more difficult.

Normandie Ides of March gaining a three-point major from Mrs. Anne Clark for owner-handler Jeanne Pierrette Dross. By Ch. Piltdown Keltic Druid ex Ch. Normandie Lady of Shars, "Ides" is linebred to Ch. Reetun's Lord Jim and Ch. Millgarth Power House, C.D.

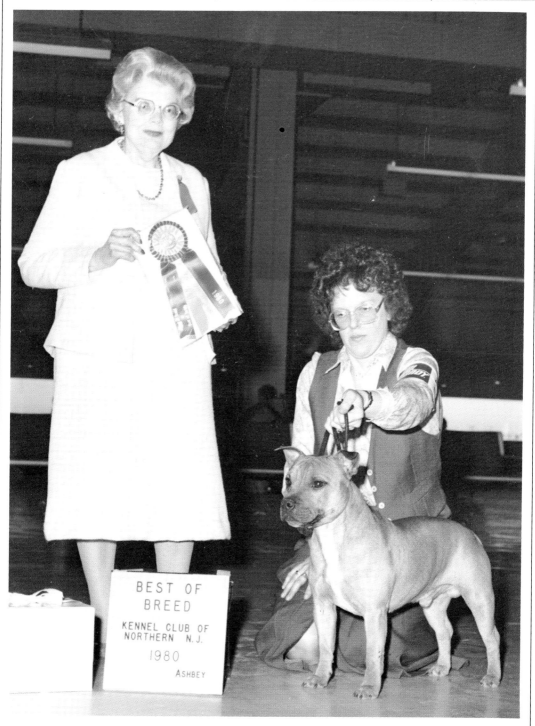

Ch. Piltdown Keltic Druid, by Eng., Am., Can., and Mex. Ch. Reetun's Lord Jim ex Piltdown St. Eve, bred by Kevin Rowland, owner-handled by Jeanne Pierrette Dross, taking Best of Breed under the author.

Your Staffordshire and Obedience

For its own protection and safety, every dog should be taught, at the very least, to recognize and obey the commands "Come," "Heel," "Down," "Sit," and "Stay." Doing so at some time might save the dog's life and in less extreme circumstances will certainly make him a better behaved, more pleasant member of society. If you are patient and enjoy working with your dog, study some of the excellent books available on the subject of obedience and then teach your canine friend these basic manners. If you need the stimulus of working with a group, find out where obedience training classes are held (usually your veterinarian, your dog's breeder, or a dog-owning friend can tell you) and you and your dog can join. Alternatively, you could let someone else do the training by sending the dog to class, but this is not very rewarding because you lose the opportunity of working with

your dog and the pleasure of the rapport thus established.

If you are going to do it yourself, there are some basic rules which you should follow. You must remain calm and confident in attitude. Never lose your temper and frighten or punish your dog unjustly. Be quick and lavish with praise each time a command is correctly followed. Make it fun for the dog and he will be eager to please you by responding correctly. Repetition is the keynote, but it should not be continued without recess to the point of tedium. Limit the training sessions to ten- or fifteen-minute periods at a time.

Formal obedience training can be followed, and very frequently is, by entering the dog in obedience competition to work toward an obedience degree, or several of them, depending on the dog's aptitude and your own enjoyment. Obedience trials are held in conjunction with the

Opposite: A most handsome headstudy of the great Am Staff winner, Ch. Iron Buck's Painted Horse, bred and owned by James and Barbara Wheat, Melrose Park, IL. An outstanding show dog and producer who has won consistently.

Top: Ch. Ledge Rock's Buck Eye Velvet during his weight-pull, November, 1984. Owned by Ernest and Ruth Prehn, Ledge Rock Kennels. *Center:* Ch. Steeltown's Blue Monday, a heart-warming Am Staff owned by Cock 'N' Bull Kennels, here serving volunteer time in a Humane Society's Animal Facilitated Therapy Program. *Bottom:* Willie Mark's Miss Orday, "Little Red" to her friends, was purchased by Dennis J. Flynn from Jim Singleton. A daughter-granddaughter of Keystone Beauregard, she was bred along lines popular with some early breeders.

majority of all-breed conformation dog shows, with Specialty shows, and frequently as separate Specialty events. If you are working alone with your dog, a list of trial dates might be obtained from your dog's veterinarian, your dog breeder, or a dog-owning friend; the AKC *Gazette* lists shows and trials to be scheduled in the coming months; and if you are a member of a training class, you will find the information readily available.

The goals for which one works in the formal AKC Member or Licensed Trials are the following titles: Companion Dog (C.D.), Companion Dog Excellent (C.D.X.), and Utility

Dog (U.D.). These degrees are earned by receiving three "legs," or qualifying scores, at each level of competition. The degrees must be earned in order, with one completed prior to starting work on the next. For example, a dog must have earned C.D. prior to starting work on C.D.X.; then

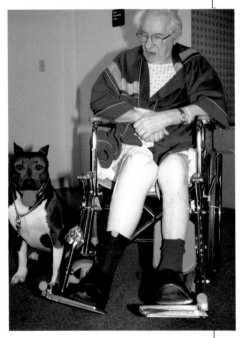

C.D.X. must be completed before U.D. work begins. The ultimate title attainable in obedience work is Obedience Trial Champion (O.T.Ch.)

When you see the letters C.D. following a dog's name, you will know that this dog has satisfactorily completed the following exercises: heel on leash and figure eight, heel free, stand for examination, recall, long sit, and long down. C.D.X. means that tests have been passed on all of those just mentioned plus heel free and figure eight, drop on recall, retrieve on flat, retrieve over high jump, broad jump, long sit, and long down. U.D. indicates that the dog has additionally passed tests in scent discrimination (leather article), scent discrimination (metal article), signal exercise, directed retrieve, directed jumping, and group stand for examination. The letters O.T.Ch. are the abbreviation for the only obedience title which precedes rather than follows a dog's name. To gain an obedience trial championship, a dog who already holds a Utility Dog degree must win a total of one hundred points and must win three firsts, under three different judges, in Utility and Open B Classes.

There is also a Tracking Dog title (T.D.) which can be earned at tracking trials. In order to pass the tracking tests the dog must follow the trail of a stranger along a path on which the trail was laid between thirty minutes and two hours previously. Along this track there must be more than two right-angle turns, at least two of which are well out in the open where no fences or other boundaries exist for the guidance of the dog or the handler. The dog wears a harness and is connected to the handler by a lead twenty to forty feet in length. Inconspicuously dropped at the end of the track is an article to be retrieved, usually a glove or wallet, which the dog is

expected to locate and the handler to pick up. The letters T.D.X. are the abbreviation for Tracking Dog Excellent, a more difficult version of the Tracking Dog test with a longer track and more turns to be worked through.

WORKING YOUR STAFFORD IN OBEDIENCE
By Faith Steinman

Ch. Kinder's Blue at WildWind, by Ch. Patton's Red Rocket ex Kinder's Little Kay. Bred by Karen Kinder of California and owned by Chet and Lauraine Rodgers, this bitch is strong in Patton's breeding.

Whether you buy your Staffordshire Bull Terrier to show in competition obedience, or as a family member, or as a contender in conformation classes, some sort of training is essential. That cute little puppy will grow up to become a very strong, muscular animal, and without early training will surely be a handful for even an experienced dog owner.

The Staffordshire Bull Terrier is generally good with

The patriotic and obedient Cock 'N' Bull's Ch. Steeltown's Blue Monday with "All-American" Patrick Julian Brown. Owners, Jerry E. and Julianna A. Brown.

people. The problem may come in when he is exposed to other animals. *He will not initiate a fight.* Rather, the aggression comes when he is challenged by another dog.

By exposing your Staff to other dogs through early training (the obedience class offers this), you can control this aggression as the puppy grows. He learns early on that unprovoked aggression is not allowed. This does not break his spirit, nor tone down his "Staffiness." It just teaches him

plain good manners.

My first Stafford was Pumptail Dragonstar Dancer. She came to live with me in December 1980 at the age of nine months. She wasn't bold, she was rather quiet and laid back for several days. She must have missed her breeder and his family, for she sat in the corner of the kitchen and had to be coaxed out even for dinner. My children asked, "Will she live in that corner all her life, Mom?" Then after several days, she started to make

herself right at home and the kids in my household were delighted. She would chase a ball and play tug of war for as long as someone had time for her. Active and agile was my little girl!

The dog training club in my town had an ad running in the local paper stating that training classes were to start in January. Now in my area, January is not the month in which to do heeling outside. The snow was so deep that poor Dancer's belly scraped along the top. She came from Arizona. *Snow—What's That?!*

We made it through the first ten weeks of training. Our instructor for the session was a very unyielding lady who would shout signals like a Marine drill sargeant. If you had not practiced your lesson for the week, there was no fooling her. So each week Dancer and I would practice our lesson for ten minutes twice each day. That was 20 minutes I could get away from the household chores and my children and spend with my dear friend. Many times it was a welcome change of pace; other times it was a chore to drag my tired body off my easy chair. If someone tells you that dog training is easy, don't believe them. It is hard work, but the rewards are many. Despite the hard work, we did enjoy seeing the results of our labor and decided to take an advanced class. This time, the weather was just a little warmer as winter yielded to spring, and

Ch. Cresstock Necromancer, C.D., by Ch. Silverlake Hurricane ex Ch. Cresstock Delight, was bred by Bonnie Cresse and is owned by Kriss Richards, Salt Lake City, UT. Shown here with medallions and a trophy for High Scoring Terrier in Trial, earned en route to his C.D. title.

we could do so much more outside. We sought out distractions such as the neighborhood playground, and the Jewel food store with all the rattling carts and swinging, hissing automatic doors, cars coming and going, running noisy kids, and lots of other foreign noises.

Most people bring their dogs to training class to have them learn a few simple things. They want their dogs to heel at their side without dragging them down the road, which, considering how strong Staffordshires are, is most important. To come when called, which could save your dog's life in certain circumstances, is the hardest exercise to teach *any* dog, for once free of restraint, he will no longer have to pay attention to you. Staffs are very quick and love to run free to chase cats and squirrels. Other training class exercises, the sit-stay and the down-stay, when taught reliably, will allow you the freedom of leaving your dog

Ch. Guardstock's Witches Double, born February, 1982, was bred by Ed and Darlene Strand and is owned by D.L. "Jim" Davenport, of Sun Valley, CA. By Guardstock's Diamond Warrior (Darton of Henstaff ex Wystaff Witchcraft) ex Wystaff Witchcraft (Ch. Wystaff Warlock ex Wystaff Wicked Lady), this SBT is being used very successfully in the Davenhill breeding program.

and returning to find her in the same spot you left her. These exercises are a great way for all Staffs to learn self-control. For the person wanting a family pet, this much training is sufficient to insure your Staff of becoming a good canine citizen.

The person wanting to enter the field of competition obedience will find the road to a utility degree is far from simple. Competition obedience is not easy for a breed such as the sporting dog, whose natural ability is to retrieve and to return. So a Staff, with no natural instinct toward retrieving, is twice as tough to teach. Their tolerance to pain (as when using the ear pinch) is in my opinion the only reliable method to teach the retrieve and is a humbling experience. I have spent as much as 15 minutes crawling on my knees (this is where my housemaid knees come from, not scrubbing the floor) or bending at the waist in a battle of wits to see who would be the

victor—Dancer not retrieving the dumbbell or myself ending the exercise with the dumbbell successfully in her mouth.

This scenario is repeated with each new exercise taught. Who will win? Staffs love to please, but hate being forced into it. I firmly believe that is the reason *bull* was included in their name. It takes a *firm* but *loving* hand to teach any dog, especially a Staff. Firm does *not* mean *violent*. It means having a stronger will than your Staff. An angry tone of voice can accomplish more than physical force. I have found that taking the dog's jowls in both hands and looking her straight in the eyes and scolding her is much more effective than any physical force you could use when the stubborn bull comes out in a negative way. Teaching the word *no* to a young puppy with this method will enable you to be the dominant figure in its life. In the wild, every pack has a leader, and you must be the leader *now*, while she is young, in order to maintain control as she grows older and stronger.

That nice, easygoing, very tolerant puppy will change her attitude around the age of two years. At this time you may see her showing more aggression— not meanness, just bull-headedness. Once they are taught anything, Staffs will not forget, owing to their high degree of intelligence.

Working on my second obedience dog, I had paved the way a lot earlier to my Utility

The United American Staffordshire Terrier Club Obedience Team. Left to right, handlers and dogs include: Ed Heaton with Ch. Steeltown's Diamond Boy and Cock 'N' Bull's Poppycock, C.D.; Delphine Heaton with Steeltown's Almost An Angel, C.D.; Julianna A. Brown with Cock 'N' Bull's Blu Pauly; Tami Teal with Chikako I'm A Black Katoo; and Mike Teal with Ch. Chikako Black and White Tatoo, C.D. Mr. Dick Koehler is the instructor.

degree with conditioning, trust, and knowledge. Being told that with each dog it gets easier, I have now learned that to be the truth. After the hard training and problems encountered with the first dog, there is no greater thrill than having the next one qualify for a leg and realize that you have just placed in your class among three Golden Retrievers. Just like raising children, with each dog it gets easier, as the mistakes made with the first dog can be avoided with the second.

My experience with showing my Staff Bulls in the obedience ring has brought about a greater respect for the breed by the judges, other exhibitors, and the spectators from outside the ring. Our goal is hopefully to educate everyone with whom we come in contact that a Staff Bull, when given the proper training for home or competition, can be a very loving and gentle animal. People will realize that they do not deserve the adverse publicity they have received in some quarters!

Author's Note: *Mrs. Steinman has written these comments as the owner of Staffordshire Bull Terriers who have been successful in competition obedience. Her experiences with Staffordshire Bull Terriers are, it is certain, equally applicable to American Staffordshires.*

Breeding Your Staffordshire

The first responsibility of any person breeding dogs is to do so with care, forethought, and deliberation. It is inexcusable to breed more litters than you need to carry on your show program or to perpetuate your bloodlines. A responsible breeder should not cause a litter to be born without definite plans for the safe and happy disposition of the puppies.

A responsible dog breeder makes absolutely certain, so far as is humanly possible, that the home to which one of his puppies will go is a good home, one that offers proper care and an enthusiastic owner. To be admired are those breeders who insist on visiting (although doing so is not always feasible) the prospective owners of their puppies to see if they have suitable facilities for keeping a dog, to find out if they understand the responsibility involved, and to make certain if all members of the household are in accord regarding the desirability of owning one. All breeders should carefully check out the credentials of prospective purchasers to be sure that the puppy is being placed in responsible hands.

No breeder ever wants a puppy or grown dog he has raised to wind up in an animal shelter, in an experimental laboratory, or as a victim of a speeding car. While complete control of such a situation may be impossible, it is important to make every effort to turn over dogs to responsible people. When selling a puppy, it is a good idea to do so with the understanding that should it become necessary to place the dog in other hands, the purchaser will first contact you, the breeder. You may want to help in some way, possibly by buying or taking back the dog or placing it elsewhere. It is not fair to sell puppies and then never again give a thought to their welfare. Family problems

Opposite: This handsome Am Staff, by Ch. Sertoma's Blaze ex Ch. Stafford's Nitro Darcas, is Ch. Bayshire's Medallion, C.D., who was owner-bred by James and Nancy Bullock, Rogersville, MO.

This handsome winning Am Staff is Dancinsun's Lord Gretsch taking Winners Dog in a large entry at the Delaware Water Gap in 1986, under the author. Born in June, 1985, he is a son of Ch. Kaufman's Koko King ex Barway's Pick Pocket, was bred by Paula Bright, Dancinsun's Kennels, Portsmouth, VA. Handled here by Tom Frampton. Owners, John R. and Louann C. Dittbredder and Paula Bright.

arise, people may be forced to move where dogs are prohibited, or people just grow bored with a dog and its care. Thus the dog becomes a victim. You, as the dog's breeder, should concern yourself with the welfare of each of your dogs and see to it that the dog remains in good hands.

The final obligation every dog owner shares, be there just one dog or an entire kennel involved, is that of making detailed, explicit plans for the future of these dearly loved animals in the event of the owner's death. Far too many people are apt to procrastinate and leave this very important matter unattended to, feeling that everything will work out or that "someone will see to them." Neither is too likely, at least not to the benefit of the dogs, unless you have done some advance planning which will assure their future well-being.

Life is filled with the

unexpected, and even the youngest, healthiest, most robust of us may be the victim of a fatal accident or sudden illness. The fate of your dogs, so entirely in your hands, should never be left to chance. If you have not already done so, please get together with your lawyer and set up a clause in your will specifying what you want done with each of your dogs, to whom they will be entrusted (after first making absolutely certain that the person selected is willing and able to assume the responsibility), and telling the locations of all registration papers, pedigrees, and kennel records. Just think of the possibilities which might happen otherwise! If there is another family member who shares your love of the dogs, that is good and you have less to worry about. But if your heirs are not dog-oriented, they will hardly know how to proceed or how to cope with the dogs themselves, and they may wind up disposing of or caring for your dogs in a manner that would break your heart were you around to know about it.

It is advisable to have in your will specific instructions concerning each of your dogs. A friend, also a dog person who regards his or her own dogs with the same concern and esteem as you do, may agree to take over their care until they can be placed accordingly and will make certain that all will work out as you have planned.

This person's name and phone number can be prominently displayed in your van or car and in your wallet. Your lawyer can be made aware of this fact. This can be spelled out in your will. The friend can have a signed check of yours to be used in case of an emergency or accident when you are traveling with the dogs; this check can be used to cover his or her expense to come and take over the care of your dogs should anything happen to make it impossible for you to do so. This is the least any dog owner should do

Ch. Cresstock Hot Item, by Silverlake Hurricane ex Ch. Cresstock Delight, was bred by Bonnie Cresse and is owned by Melvin Webb. Here winning Best of Breed at Idaho Capitol City K.C., 1983.

in preparation for the time their dogs suddenly find themselves alone. There have been so many sad cases of dogs unprovided for by their loving owners, left to heirs who couldn't care less and who disposed of them in any way at all to get rid of them, or left to heirs who kept and neglected them under the misguided idea that they were providing them "a fine home with lots of freedom." These misfortunes must be prevented from befalling your own dogs who have meant so much you!

Conscientious breeders feel quite strongly that the only possible reason for producing puppies is the ambition to improve and uphold quality and temperament within the breed—definitely *not* because one hopes to make a quick cash profit on a mediocre litter, which never seems to work out that way in the long run and which accomplishes little beyond perhaps adding to the nation's heartbreaking number of unwanted canines. The only reason ever for breeding a litter is, with conscientious people, a desire to improve the quality of dogs in their own kennel or, as pet owners, to add to the number of dogs they themselves own with a puppy or two from their present favorites. In either case, breeding should not take place unless one definitely has prospective owners for as many puppies as the litter may contain, lest you find yourself with several fast-growing young dogs and no homes in which to place them.

THE BROOD BITCH

Bitches should not be mated earlier than their second season, by which time they should be from fifteen to eighteen months old. Many breeders prefer to wait and finish the championships of their show bitches before breeding them, as pregnancy can be a disaster to a show coat and getting the bitch back in shape again takes time. When you have decided what will be the proper time, start watching at least several months ahead for what you feel would be the perfect mate to best complement your bitch's quality and bloodlines. Subscribe to the magazines which feature your breed

The multiple Group-placing import Reetun's Rufus The Red is one year old in this photo. Owned and handled by J. Zane Smith.

MISSISSIPPI COAST

the quality of the puppies from bitches with backgrounds similar to your bitch's. If the puppies have been of the type and quality you admire, then this dog would seem a sensible choice for yours, too.

Stud fees may be a few hundred dollars, sometimes even more under special situations for a particularly successful sire. It is money well spent, however. *Do not* ever breed to a dog because he is less expensive than the others unless you honestly believe that he can sire the kind of puppies who will be a credit to your kennel and your breed.

Contacting the owners of the stud dogs you find interesting will bring you pedigrees and pictures which you can then study in relation to your bitch's pedigree and conformation. Discuss your plans with other breeders who are knowledgeable (including the one who bred your own bitch). You may not always receive an entirely unbiased opinion (particularly if the person giving it also has an available stud dog), but one learns by discussion so listen to what they say, consider their opinions, and then you may be better qualified to form your own opinion.

As soon as you have made a choice, phone the owner of the stud dog you wish to use to find out if this will be agreeable. You will be asked about the bitch's health, soundness, temperament, and freedom from serious faults. A copy of

Ch. Guardsman's Red Atom, an attractive SBT placing at Mississippi Coast K.C. Owners, Judi Daniels and Joe LeBlanc.

exclusively and to some which cover all breeds in order to familiarize yourself with outstanding stud dogs in areas other than your own, for there is no necessity nowadays to limit your choice to a local dog unless you truly like him and feel that he is the most suitable. It is quite usual to ship a bitch to a stud dog a distance away, and this generally works out with no ill effects. The important thing is that you need a stud dog strong in those features where your bitch is weak, a dog whose bloodlines are compatible with hers. Compare the background of both your bitch and the stud dog under consideration, paying particular attention to

Kar-Ron Finwar's Success, owned by Karen and Ron Tucker of Pennsburg, PA. Winning Puppy Group First at the Delaware Water Gap Match Show, 1986.

her pedigree may be requested, as might a picture of her. A discussion of her background over the telephone may be sufficient to assure the stud's owner that she is suitable for the stud dog and that she is of type, breeding, and quality herself, capable of producing the kind of puppies for which the stud is noted. The owner of a top-quality stud is often extremely selective in the bitches permitted to be bred to his dog, in an effort to keep the standard of his puppies high. The owner of a stud dog may require that the bitch be tested for brucellosis, which should be attended to not more than a month previous to the breeding.

Check out which airport will be most convenient for the person meeting and returning the bitch, if she is to be shipped, and also what airlines use that airport. You will find that the airlines are also apt to have special requirements concerning acceptance of animals for shipping. These include weather limitations and types of crates which are acceptable. The weather limits have to do with extreme heat and extreme cold at the point of destination, as some airlines will not fly dogs into temperatures above or below certain levels, fearing for their safety. The crate problem is a simple one, since, if your own crate is not suitable, most of the airlines have specially designed crates available for purchase at a fair and moderate price. It is a good plan to purchase one of these if you intend to be shipping dogs with any sort of frequency. They are made of fiberglass and are the safest type to use for shipping.

Normally you must notify the airline several days in advance to make a reservation, as they are able to accommodate only a certain number of dogs on each flight. Plan on shipping the bitch on about her eighth or ninth day of season, but be careful to avoid shipping her on a weekend when schedules often vary and freight offices are apt to be closed. Whenever you can, ship your bitch on a direct flight. Changing planes always carries a certain amount of risk of a dog being overlooked or wrongly routed at the middle stop, so avoid this danger if at all possible. The bitch must be accompanied by a health certificate which you must obtain from your veterinarian before taking her to the airport. Usually it will be necessary to have the bitch at the airport about two hours prior to flight time. Before finalizing arrangements, find out from

Ch. Diamonds Crystal of Kar-Ron, by Ch. Tryarr Diamondback Redbolt ex Ch. Tryarr Wonderful You, is owned by Ron and Karen Tucker. Born January, 1982, "Crystal" was bred by Thomas Shimak. Here winning Best of Breed at Bronx County, 1983, under the author.

the stud's owner at what time of day it will be most convenient to have the bitch picked up promptly upon arrival.

It is simpler if you can bring the bitch to the stud dog yourself. Some people feel that the trauma of the flight may cause the bitch to not conceive; and, of course, undeniably there is a slight risk in shipping which can be avoided if you are able to drive the bitch to her destination. Be sure to leave yourself sufficient time to assure your arrival at the right time for her for breeding

Ch. Davenhill's Rikki Tikki, born in 1980, a daughter of Ch. Wystaff Wrecker ex Ch. Silverlake Gemstock. Bred by D.L. Davenport. Owned by Stan Thorn, Greenwood Springs, MS.

(normally the tenth to fourteenth day following the first signs of color); and remember that if you want the bitch bred twice, you should allow a day to elapse between the two matings. Do not expect the stud's owner to house you while you are there. Locate a nearby motel that takes dogs and make that your headquarters.

Just prior to the time your bitch is due in season, you should take her to visit your veterinarian. She should be checked for worms and should receive all the booster shots for which she is due plus one for parvovirus, unless she has had the latter shot fairly recently. The brucellosis test can also be done then, and the health certificate can be obtained for shipping if she is to travel by air. Should the bitch be at all overweight, now is the time to get the surplus off. She should be in good condition, neither underweight nor overweight, at the time of breeding.

The moment you notice the swelling of the vulva, for which you should be checking daily as the time for her season approaches, and the appearance of color, immediately contact the stud's owner and settle on the day for shipping or make the appointment for your arrival with the bitch for breeding. If you are shipping the bitch, the stud fee check should be mailed immediately, leaving ample time for it to have been received when the bitch arrives and the mating takes place. Be sure to call the airline, making her reservation at that time, too.

Do not feed the bitch within a few hours before shipping her. Be certain that she has had a drink of water and been well exercised before closing her in the crate. Several layers of newspapers, topped with some shredded newspaper, make a good bed and can be discarded

Ch. Davenhill Silverlake Lisa, born February, 1976. A daughter of Ch. Silverzend Satan ex Ch. Sliverlake Gemstock. Bred by Lillian Rant and D.L. Davenport. Owned by D.L. "Jim" Davenport.

when she arrives at her destination; these can be replaced with fresh newspapers for her return home. Remember that the bitch should be brought to the airport about two hours before flight time, as sometimes the airlines refuse to accept late arrivals.

If you are taking your bitch by car, be certain that you will arrive at a reasonable time of day. Do not appear late in the evening. If your arrival in town is not until late, get a good night's sleep at your motel and contact the stud's owner first thing in the morning. If possible, leave children and relatives at home, as they will only be in the way and perhaps unwelcome by the stud's owner. Most stud dog owners prefer not to have any unnecessary people on hand during the actual mating.

After the breeding has taken place, if you wish to sit and visit for awhile and the stud's owner has the time, return the bitch to her crate in your car

(first ascertaining, of course, that the temperature is comfortable for her and that there is proper ventilation). She should not be permitted to urinate for at least one hour following the breeding. This is the time when you attend to the business part of the transaction. Pay the stud fee, upon which you should receive your breeding certificate and, if you do not already have it, a copy of the stud dog's pedigree. The owner of the stud dog does not sign or furnish a litter registration application until the puppies have been born.

Upon your return home, you can settle down and plan in happy anticipation a wonderful litter of puppies. A word of caution! Remember that although she has been bred, your bitch is still an interesting target for all male dogs, so guard her carefully for the next week or until you are absolutely certain that her season has entirely ended. This would be no time to have any

Ch. Coalminer's Mystery Man with a friend. Many Staffordshire Bull Terriers and Doberman Pinchers do not have problems getting along together. "Maestro" belongs to Tracy Dineley.

Eva Lydick owns this handsome puppy, "Star," obviously already a well-adjusted bedfellow.

unfortunate incident with another dog.

THE STUD DOG

Choosing the best stud dog to complement your bitch is often very difficult. The two principal factors to be considered should be the stud's conformation and his pedigree. Conformation is fairly obvious; you want a dog that is typical of the breed in the words of the Standard of perfection. Understanding pedigrees is a bit more subtle since the pedigree lists the ancestry of the dog and involves individuals and bloodlines with which you may not be entirely familiar.

To a novice in the breed, the correct interpretation of a pedigree may at first be difficult to grasp. Study the pictures and text of this book and you will find many names of important bloodlines and members of the breed. Also make an effort to discuss the various dogs behind the

proposed stud with some of the more experienced breeders, starting with the breeder of your own bitch. Frequently these folks will be familiar with many of the dogs in question, will be able to offer opinions of them, and may have access to additional pictures which you would benefit by seeing. It is very important that the stud's pedigree be harmonious with that of the bitch you plan on breeding to him. Do not rush out and breed to the latest winner with no thought of whether or not he can produce true quality. By no means are all great show dogs great producers. It is the producing record of the dog in question, and the dogs and bitches from which he has come, that should be the basis on which you make your choice.

Breeding dogs is never a money-making operation. By the time you pay a stud fee, care for the bitch during pregnancy, whelp the litter, and rear the puppies through their early shots, worming, and so on, you will be fortunate to break even financially once the puppies have been sold. Your chances of doing this are greater if you are breeding for a show-quality litter which will bring you higher prices, as the pups are sold as show prospects. Therefore, your wisest investment is to use the best dog available for your bitch regardless of the cost; then you should wind up with more valuable puppies. Remember that it is equally costly to raise mediocre puppies as it is top ones, and your chances of financial return are better on the latter. Breeding to the most excellent, most suitable stud dog you can find is the only sensible thing to do, and it is poor economy to quibble over the amount you are paying in a stud fee.

It will be your decision as to which course you follow when you breed your bitch, as there are three options: linebreeding, inbreeding, and outcrossing. Each of these methods has its supporters and its detractors! Linebreeding is breeding a bitch to a dog belonging originally to the same canine family, being descended from the same ancestors, such as half brother to half sister, grandsire to granddaughter, niece to uncle (and vice-versa) or cousin to cousin. Inbreeding is breeding father to daughter, mother to son, or full brother to sister. Outcross breeding is breeding a dog and a bitch with no or only a few mutual ancestors.

Ch. Kodiak's Blue Haze pictured finishing title at age seven months in Montgomery County after a victorious three-show weekend. By Ch. Aranda Angelina V. Kodiak ex Ch. Byron's Finn McCool, "Blue Haze" is owned by Fred and Sharon Marushak, Quakertown, PA.

Linebreeding is probably the safest course, and the one most likely to bring results, for the novice breeder. The more sophisticated inbreeding should be left to the experienced, longtime breeders who throroughly know and understand the risks and the possibilities involved with a particular line. It is usually done in an effort to intensify some ideal feature in that strain. Outcrossing is the reverse of inbreeding, an effort to introduce improvement in a specific feature needing correction, such as a shorter back, better movement, more correct head or coat, and so on.

Top: Ch. Loggerhead's Gaylord gained his American title in six shows, finishing here by taking Best of Winners for five points at Starved Rock K.C. in July, 1986; owner-handled by Joe LeBlanc. "Gaylord" is the last SBT to carry the Loggerhead prefix, the only one in his litter. *Bottom:* Ka Nakht Moss Rose (eight points, both "majors") and Ch. Ka Nakht Jack O'Diamonds, Top Dog, 1982. Moss Rose is owned by Nancy Lee of Najan's Staffords, and Jack O'Diamonds is owned by Cindy Crawford of Dragonquest Kennels. The breeder of both dogs is Mrs. Barbara Elder.

Ch. Piltdown Keltic Druid at 15 months of age receiving his first Group placement, a third, at St. Lawrence Valley Dog Club, June 2, 1979. Judge, Ms. Florise Hogan. Owner-handler, Jeanne Pierrette Dross of Albany, NY.

Ch. Ledge Rock's Buckeye Velvet, an Am Staff owned and bred by Ernest and Ruth Prehn of Ledge Rock Kennels.

It is the serious breeder's ambition to develop a strain or bloodline of their own, one strong in qualities for which their dogs will become distinguished. However, it must be realized that this will involve time, patience, and at least several generations before the achievement can be claimed. The safest way to embark on this plan, as previously mentioned, is by the selection and breeding of one or two bitches, the best you can buy and from top-producing kennels. In the beginning you do *not* really have to own a stud dog. In the long run it is less

expensive and sounder judgement to pay a stud fee when you are ready to breed a bitch than to purchase a stud dog and feed him all year; a stud dog does not win any popularity contests with owners of bitches to be bred until he becomes a champion, has been successfully Specialed for a while, and has been at least moderately advertised, all of which adds up to quite a healthy expenditure.

The wisest course for the inexperienced breeder just starting out in dogs is to keep the best bitch puppy from the first several litters. After that you may wish to consider keeping your own stud dog, if there has been a particularly handsome male in one of your litters that you feel has great potential or if you know where there is one available that you are interested in, with the feeling that he would work in nicely with the breeding program on which you have embarked. By this time, with several litters already born, your eye should have developed to a point enabling you to make a wise choice, either from one of your own litters or from among dogs you have seen that appear suitable.

The greatest care should be taken in the selection of your own stud dog. He must be of true type and highest quality as he may be responsible for siring many puppies each year, and he should come from a line of excellent dogs on both sides of his pedigree which themselves are, and which are descended from, successful producers. This dog should have no glaring faults in conformation; he should be of such quality that he can hold his own in keenest competition within his breed. He should be in good health, be virile and be a keen stud dog, a proven sire able to transmit his correct qualities to his puppies. Need one say that such a dog will be enormously expensive unless you have the good fortune to produce him in one of your own litters? To buy and use a lesser stud dog, however, is downgrading your breeding program unnecessarily since there are so many dogs fitting the description of a fine stud whose services can be used on payment of a stud fee.

You should *never* breed to an unsound dog or one with any serious disqualifying faults according to the breed's standard. Not all champions by any means pass along their best features; and by the same token, occasionally you will find a great one who can pass along his best features but never gained his championship title due to some unusual circumstances. The information you need about a stud dog is what type of puppies he has produced, and with what bloodlines, and whether or not he possesses the bloodlines and attributes considered characteristic of the best in your breed.

If you go out to buy a stud dog, obviously he will not be a puppy, but rather a fully mature and proven male with as many of the best attributes as possible. True, he will be an expensive investment, but if you choose and make his selection with care and forethought, he may well prove to be one of the best investments you have ever made.

Of course, the most exciting of all is when a young male you have decided to keep from one of your litters, due to his tremendous show potential, turns out to be a stud dog such as we have described. In this case he should be managed with care, for he is a valuable

Am Staff, Ch. Willynwood Velvet Shadow, C.D., handled by Carolyn Kinley. Owned by Ernest and Ruth Prehn.

Ch. Davenhill's Firebrewed Brody, by Ch. Starzend Zodiac Force ex Ch. Guardstock's Witches Double, finished his title at age nine months. Brody is a great-grandson of the original stock through Ch. Silverzend Satan.

property that can contribute inestimably to this breed as a whole and to your own kennel specifically.

Do not permit your stud dog to be used until he is about a year old, and even then he should be bred to a mature, proven matron accustomed to breeding who will make his first experience pleasant and easy. A young dog can be put off forever by a maiden bitch who fights and resists his advances. Never allow this to happen. Always start a stud dog out with a bitch who is mature, has been bred previously, and is of even temperament. The first breeding should be performed in quiet surroundings with only you and one other person to hold the bitch. Do not make it a circus, as the experience will determine the dog's outlook about future stud work. If he does not enjoy the first experience or associates it with

any unpleasantness, you may well have a problem in the future.

Your young stud must permit help with the breeding, as later there will be bitches who will not be cooperative. If right from the beginning you are there helping him and praising him, whether or not your assistance is actually needed, he will expect and accept this as a matter of course when a difficult bitch comes along.

Things to have handy before introducing your dog and the bitch are K-Y jelly (the only lubricant which should be used) and a length of gauze with which to muzzle the bitch should it be necessary to keep her from biting you or the dog. Some bitches put up a fight; others are calm. It is best to be prepared.

At the time of the breeding, the stud fee comes due, and it is expected that it will be paid promptly. Normally a return service is offered in case the bitch misses or fails to produce one live puppy. Conditions of the service are what the stud dog's owner makes them, and there are no standard rules covering this. The stud fee is paid for the act, not the result. If the bitch fails to conceive, it is customary for the owner to offer a free return service; but this is a courtesy and not to be considered a right, particularly in the case of a proven stud who is siring consistently and whose fault the failure obviously is *not*. Stud dog owners are always anxious to

Kar-Ron Komet of Ledge Rock, age seven months, Sweepstakes Winner, Associated Terrier Club, February, 1986. Bred by Ron and Karen Tucker. Handled by William Thompson. Owned by Ernest and Ruth Prehn. "Komet" is by Ch. Ledge Rock's Kopper Korn ex Ch. Diamonds Crystal of Kar-Ron. Judge here is Lina Basquette.

see their clients get good value and to have, in the ring, winning young stock by their dog; therefore, very few refuse to mate the second time. It is wise, however, for both parties to have the terms of the transaction clearly understood at the time of the breeding.

If the return service has been provided and the bitch has missed a second time, that is considered to be the end of the matter and the owner would be expected to pay a further fee if it is felt that the bitch should be given a third chance with the stud dog. The management of a stud dog and his visiting bitches is quite a task, and a stud fee has usually been well earned when one service has been achieved, let alone by repeated visits from the same bitch.

The accepted litter is one live puppy. It is wise to have printed a breeding certificate which the owner of the stud dog and the owner of the bitch both sign. This should list in detail the conditions of the breeding as well as the dates of the mating.

Upon occasion, arrangements other than a stud fee in cash are made for a breeding, such as the owner of the stud taking a pick-of-the-litter puppy in lieu of money. This should be

Ch. Aranda Angelina V. Kodiak, by Ch. Sir Vessa ex Ch. Barway's Chantilly Lace V. Aranda. Born January, 1983. Pictured at age eight months, two months prior to completion of championship with multiple Bests of Breed and Bests of Opposite Sex over "Specials." Owned by Fred and Sharon Marushak of the Kodiak Kennels.

clearly specified on the breeding certificate along with the terms of the age at which the stud's owner will select the puppy, whether it is to be a specific sex, or whether it is to be the pick of the entire litter.

The price of a stud fee varies according to circumstances. Usually, to prove a young stud dog, his owner will allow the first breeding to be quite inexpensive. Then, once a bitch has become pregnant by him, he becomes a "proven stud"

and the fee rises accordingly for bitches that follow. The sire of championship quality puppies will bring a stud fee of at least the purchase price of one show puppy as the accepted "rule-of-thumb." Until at least one champion by your stud dog has finished, the fee will remain equal to the price of one pet puppy. When his list of champions starts to grow, so does the amount of the stud fee. For a top-producing sire of champions, the stud fee will rise accordingly.

Almost invariably it is the bitch who comes to the stud dog for the breeding. Immediately upon having selected the stud dog you wish to use, discuss the possibility with the owner of that dog. It is the stud dog owner's prerogative to refuse to breed any bitch deemed unsuitable for this dog. Stud fee and method of payment should be stated at this time and a decision reached on whether it is to be a full cash transaction at the time of the mating or a pick-of-the-litter puppy, usually at eight weeks of age.

If the owner of the stud dog must travel to an airport to meet the bitch and ship her for the flight home, an additional charge will be made for time, tolls, and gasoline based on the stud owner's proximity to the airport. The stud fee includes board for the day on the bitch's arrival through two days for breeding, with a day in between. If it is necessary that the bitch remain longer, it is

Ch. Sooner's Cherokee Strip, an impressive and handsome dog by Ch. Sooner's Big Mac ex Ch. Midnight. Bred by Elmer Parsons. Photo courtesy of Lenna Hanna.

Ch. Kar-Ron Crystals Lil' Engorcer, owned by Karen Tucker, taking Best of Winners at Penn Treaty in 1985.

very likely that additional board will be charged at the normal per-day rate for the breed.

Be sure to advise the stud's owner as soon as you know that your bitch is in season so that the stud dog will be available. This is especially important because if he is a dog being shown, he and his owner may be unavailable, owing to the dog's absence from home.

As the owner of a stud dog being offered to the public, it is essential that you have proper facilities for the care of visiting bitches. Nothing can be worse than a bitch being insecurely housed and slipping out to become lost or bred by the wrong dog. If you are taking people's valued bitches into

your kennel or home, it is imperative that you provide them with comfortable, secure housing and good care while they are your responsibility.

There is no dog more valuable than the proven sire of champions, Group winners, and Best in Show dogs. Once you have such an animal, guard his reputation well and do *not* permit him to be bred to just any bitch that comes along. It takes two to make the puppies; even the most dominant stud cannot do it all himself, so never permit him to breed a bitch you consider unworthy. Remember that when the puppies arrive, it will be your stud dog who will be blamed for any lack of quality, while the bitch's shortcomings will be quickly and conveniently overlooked.

Going into the actual management of the mating is a bit superfluous here. If you have had previous experience in breeding a dog and bitch, you will know how the mating is done. If you do not have such experience, you should not attempt to follow directions given in a book but should have a veterinarian, breeder friend, or handler there to help you with the first few times. You do not turn the dog and bitch loose together and await developments, as too many things can go wrong and you may altogether miss getting the bitch bred. Someone should hold the dog and the bitch (one person each) until the "tie" is made and these two people should stay with them during the entire act.

If you get a complete tie, probably only the one mating is absolutely necessary. However, especially with a maiden bitch or one that has come a long distance for this breeding, a

Ch. Coalminer's Mystery Man, by Topcroft Minstrel ex Ch. Peck's Sexy Pants, is owner-handled to Group placement here by Tracy Dineley, Clandara Kennels, Ontario, Canada. Bred by Evelyn Frei.

Ch. Sooner's Cherokee Strip checks a most charming litter of Am Staff pups. Photo courtesy of Lenna S. Hanna.

follow-up with a second breeding is preferred, leaving one day in between the two matings. In this way there will be little or no chance of the bitch missing.

Once the tie has been completed and the dogs release, be certain that the male's penis goes completely back within its sheath. He should be allowed a drink of water and a short walk, and then he should be put into his crate or somewhere alone where he can settle down. Do not allow him to be with other dogs for a while as they will notice the odor of the bitch on him, and, particularly with other males present, he may become involved in a fight.

PREGNANCY, WHELPING, AND THE LITTER

Once the bitch has been bred and is back at home, remember to keep an ever watchful eye that no other males get to her until at least the twenty-second day of her season has passed. Until then, it will still be possible for an unwanted breeding to take place, which at this point would be

Top: Ch. Piltdown Mata Hari, No. 1 Staffordshire Bull Terrier Bitch in the U.S. for 1982, All-Systems. A multiple Best of Breed winner, bred by Ed Rowland and owned by J. Zane Smith. A daughter of Ch. Piltdown Luigi Marano ex Ch. Rannvans Pride of Rannoch. *Bottom:* Ch. Cresstock Our Tawny, by Ch. Cresstock Logo of Linden ex Starzend Trugrip Naughty, winning Best of Breed at Idaho Capitol City in 1985. Bred by Bob and Diane Ongerand, and owned by Bonnie Cresse of Cresstock Kennels.

221

catastrophic. Remember that she actually can have two separate litters by two different dogs, so take care.

In other ways, she should be treated normally. Controlled exercise is good and necessary for the bitch throughout her pregnancy, tapering it off to just several short walks daily, preferably on lead, as she reaches her seventh week. As her time grows close, be careful about her jumping or playing too roughly.

The theory that a bitch should be overstuffed with food when pregnant is a poor one. A fat bitch is never an easy whelper, so the overfeeding you consider good for her may well turn out to be a hindrance later on. During the first few weeks of pregnancy, your bitch should be fed her normal diet. At four to five weeks along, calcium should be added to her food. At seven weeks her food may be increased if she seems to crave more than she is getting, and a

Ch. Ledge Rock's Kopper Korn, Best of Winners at the AKC Centennial Show, November, 1984, at age 15 months. Pictured with owner Ruth Prehn of Ledge Rock Kennels. This magnificent Am Staff finished with two five-point majors. Born August 30, 1983, he is the foundation stud at Ledge Rock.

Ch. Sans Tache's El Chivato at age ten months was Best of Winners at the AKC Centennial in 1984. This handsome dog is a littermate to the noted Group-winning bitch, Ch. Athenian Angel. They were sired by England's Top Staffordshire for 1981, Eng. Ch. Peg's Bolton Trip ex Kenwunn Supream. Owned by Joe LeBlanc, Sans Tache Kennels.

meal of canned milk (mixed with an equal amount of water) should be introduced. If she is fed just once a day, add another meal rather than overload her with too much at one time. If twice a day is her schedule, then a bit more food can be added to each feeding.

A week before the pups are due, your bitch should be introduced to her whelping box so that she will be accustomed to it and feel at home there when the puppies arrive. She should be encouraged to sleep there but permitted to come and go as she wishes. The box should be roomy enough for her to lie down and stretch out in but not too large, lest the pups have more room than is needed in which to roam and possibly get chilled by going too far away from their mother. Be sure that the box has a "pig rail"; this will prevent the puppies from being crushed against the sides. The room in

which the box is placed, either in your home or in the kennel, should be kept at about 70 degrees Fahrenheit. In winter it may be necessary to have an infrared lamp over the whelping box, in which case be careful not to place it too low or close to the puppies.

Newspapers will become a very important commodity, so start collecting them well in advance to have a big pile handy for the whelping box. With a litter of puppies, one never seems to have papers enough, so the higher pile to start with, the better off you will be. Other necessities for whelping time are clean, soft turkish towels, scissors, and a bottle of alcohol.

You will know that her time is very near when your bitch becomes restless, wandering in and out of her box and out of the room. She may refuse food, and at that point her temperature will start to drop.

Ch. Fraja's E.C. Dodge City wins Best of Breed under the author at Tuxedo Park K.C. 1984. John C. McCartney, Seaside Park, NJ, handling for owners Bill Olin and John King, Fraja East Coast, PA.

BEST OF BREED
TUXEDO PARK
KENNEL CLUB
1984
ASHBEY

She will dig at and tear up the newspapers in her box, shiver, and generally look uncomfortable. Only you should be with your bitch at this time. She does not need spectators; and several people hanging over her, even though they may be family members whom she knows, may upset her to the point where she may harm the puppies. You should remain nearby, quietly watching, not fussing or hovering; speak calmly and frequently to her to instill confidence. Eventually she will settle down in her box and begin panting; contractions will follow. Soon thereafter a puppy will start to emerge, sliding out with the contractions. The mother immediately should open the sac, sever the cord with her teeth, and then clean up the puppy. She will also eat the placenta, which you should permit. Once the puppy is cleaned, it should be placed next to the bitch unless she is showing signs of having the next one immediately. Almost at once the puppy will start looking for a nipple on which to nurse, and you should ascertain that it is able to latch on successfully.

If the puppy is a breech (*i.e.*, born feet first), you must watch carefully for it to be completely delivered as quickly as possible and for the sac to be removed quickly so that the puppy does not drown. Sometimes even a normally positioned birth will seem extremely slow in coming. Should this occur, you might take a clean towel, and as the bitch contracts, pull the puppy out, doing so gently and with utmost care. If, once the puppy is delivered, it shows little signs of life, take a rough turkish towel and massage the puppy's chest by rubbing quite briskly back and forth. Continue this for about fifteen minutes, and be sure that the mouth is free of liquid. It may be necessary to try mouth-to-mouth breathing, which is begun by pressing the puppy's jaws open and, using a finger, depressing the tongue which may be stuck to the roof of the mouth. Then place your mouth against the puppy's and blow hard down the puppy's throat. Rub the puppy's chest with the towel again and try artificial respiration, pressing the sides of the chest together slowly and rhythmically—in

Ch. Mother Lode Gypsophila at age 13 months. Best of Breed from the classes. She is the third SBT to have gained American-Canadian championship in the US. Owner, Dennis J. Flynn, Blue Steel Staffordshires, Dallas, TX.

and out, in and out. Keep trying one method or the other for at least twenty minutes before giving up. You may be rewarded with a live puppy who otherwise would not have made it.

If you are successful in bringing the puppy around, do not immediately put it back with the mother as it should be kept extra warm. Put it in a cardboard box on an electric

Ch. Cresstock Our Lady Goldberry taking Best of Winners en route to title at Intermountain in October, 1986. "Goldie" is a daughter of Ch. Reetun's Red Tornado ex Ch. Cresstock's Delight. Born in 1984, she is owned by Lorraine Richards of Cresstock Kennels.

heating pad or, if it is the time of year when your heat is running, near a radiator or near the fireplace or stove. As soon as the rest of the litter has been born, it then can join the others.

An hour or more may elapse between puppies, which is fine so long as the bitch seems comfortable and is neither straining nor contracting. She

should not be permitted to remain unassisted for more than an hour if she does continue to contract. This is when you should get her to your veterinarian, whom you should already have alerted to the possibility of a problem existing. He should examine her and perhaps give her a shot of Pituitrin. In some cases the veterinarian may find that a Caesarean section is necessary due to a puppy being lodged in a manner making normal delivery impossible. Sometimes this is caused by an abnormally large puppy, or it may just be that the puppy is simply turned in the wrong position. If the bitch does require a Caesarean section, the puppies already born must be kept warm in their cardboard box with a heating pad under the box.

Once the section is done, get the bitch and the puppies home. Do not attempt to put the puppies in with the bitch until she has regained consciousness, as she may unknowingly hurt them. But do get them back to her as soon as possible for them to start nursing.

Should the mother lack milk at this time, the puppies must be fed by hand, kept very warm, and held onto the mother's teats several times a day in order to stimulate and encourage the secretion of milk, which should start shortly.

Assuming that there has been no problem and that the bitch has whelped naturally, you should insist that she go out to exercise, staying just long enough to make herself comfortable. She can be offered a bowl of milk and a biscuit, but then she should settle down with her family. Freshen the whelping box for her with newspapers while she is taking this respite so that she and the puppies will have a clean bed.

Unless some problem arises, there is little you must do for the puppies until they become three to four weeks old. Keep the box clean and supplied with fresh newspapers the first few days, but then turkish towels should be tacked down to the bottom of the box so that the puppies will have traction as they move about.

If the bitch has difficulties with her milk supply, or if you should be so unfortunate as to lose her, then you must be prepared to either hand-feed or tube-feed the puppies if they are to survive. Tube-feeding is so much faster and easier. If the bitch is available, it is best that she continues to clean and care for the puppies in the normal manner, excepting for the food supplements you will provide. If it is impossible for her to do this, then after every feeding you must gently rub each puppy's abdomen with wet

Taking points on the way to title, Ch. Barker's Bug City Slicker, an outstanding winner of 1984, was bred by Linda Barker and is co-owned with Melanie Walker.

227

Right: Renowned Ch. Reetun's Lord Jim taking Best of Breed, owner-handled by J. Zane Smith, under judge D. Daniell-Jenkins. *Below:* Steeltown's Fancy Me Blue, a litter sister to Ch. Steeltown's Blue Monday, taking Best of Opposite, owner-handled by Julianna A. Brown.

cotton to make it urinate, and the rectum should be gently rubbed to open the bowels.

Newborn puppies must be fed every three to four hours around the clock. The puppies must be kept warm during this time. Have your veterinarian teach you how to tube-feed. You will find that it is really quite simple.

After a normal whelping, the bitch will require additional food to enable her to produce sufficient milk. In addition to being fed twice daily, she should be given some canned milk several times each day.

When the puppies are two weeks old, their nails should be clipped, as they are needle sharp at this age and can hurt or damage the mother's teats and stomach as the pups hold on to nurse.

Between three and four weeks of age, the puppies should begin to be weaned. Scraped beef (prepared by scraping it off slices of beef with a spoon so that none of the gristle is included) may be offered in very small quantities a couple of times daily for the first few days. Then by the third day you can mix puppy chow with warm water as directed on the package, offering it four times daily. By now the mother should be kept away from the puppies and out of the box for several hours at a time so that when they have reached five weeks of age she is left in with them only overnight. By the time the puppies are six weeks old, they should be entirely weaned and receiving only occasional visits from their mother.

Most veterinarians

Taking Best of Breed at Rio Hondo K.C., May 1986, Ch. Oltyme's Cock O' The Walk is owner-handled by Juliana A. Brown, Cock 'N' Bull Kennels.

recommend a temporary DHL (distemper, hepatitis, leptospirosis) shot when the puppies are six weeks of age. This remains effective for about two weeks. Then at eight weeks of age, the puppies should receive the series of permanent shots for DHL protection. It is also a good idea to discuss with your vet the advisability of having your puppies inoculated against the dreaded parvovirus at the same time. Each time the pups go to the vet for shots, you should bring stool samples so that they can be examined for worms. Worms go through various stages of development and may be present in a stool sample even though the sample does not test positive in every checkup. So do not neglect to keep careful watch on this.

The puppies should be fed four times daily until they are three months old. Then you can cut back to three feedings daily. By the time the puppies are six months of age, two meals daily are sufficient. Some people feed their dogs twice

Above: Kar-Ron's John Henry taking Winners Dog at the Penn Treaty K.C. in 1986. Kar-Ron American Staffordshires are owned by Karen and Ron Tucker, Pennsburg, PA.

Below: Ch. Sooner's Our Man Flint, bred by Rosanna and James Don Carlos, owner-handled by Olivia Patterson to Best of Breed from the classes, en route to his title. He is the sire of several champions.

BEST OF
WINNERS

SAW MILL
KENNEL CLUB
1986   DAVE ASHBEY

Michele Kuberski handling her successful young winner "Hacksaw" to Best of Winners at Saw Mill K.C. in 1986. A splendid young representative of the breed, Hacksaw is a son of the renowned Ch. Fraja's Thunder Battery.

daily throughout their lifetime; others go to one meal daily when the puppy becomes one year of age.

The ideal age for puppies to go to their new homes is between eight and twelve weeks, although some puppies successfully adjust to a new home when they are six weeks old. Be sure that they go to their new owners accompanied by a description of the diet you've been feeding them and a schedule of the shots they have already received and those they still need. These should be included with the registration application and a copy of the pedigree.

A CAUTION

With Staffordshires being one of the larger-headed breeds, there is always the risk of a problem in whelping. This should be discussed with your veterinarian, and plans should be made for a Caesarean should it appear that any difficulty is developing. Do not leave this to chance; make certain that your vet is available, should the need arise.

Traveling with Your Staffordshire

When you travel with your dog, to shows or on vacation or wherever, remember that everyone does not share your enthusiasm or love for dogs and that those who do not, strange creatures though they seem to us, have their rights too. These rights, on which you should not encroach, include not being disturbed, annoyed, or made uncomfortable by the presence and behavior of other people's pets. Your dog should be kept on lead in public places and should recognize and promptly obey the commands: "Down," "Come," "Sit," and "Stay."

Take along his crate if you are going any distance with your dog, and keep him in it when riding in the car. A crated dog has a far better chance of escaping injury than one riding loose in the car, should an accident occur or an emergency arise. If you do permit your dog to ride loose, never allow him to hang out a window, ears blowing in the breeze. An injury to his eyes could occur in this manner. He could also become overly excited by something he sees and jump out, or he could lose his balance and fall out.

Never, ever, under any circumstances, should a dog be permitted to ride loose in the back of a pick-up truck. Some people do transport dogs in this manner, which is cruel and shocking. How easily such a dog can be thrown out of the truck by sudden jolts or an impact! Doubtless many dogs have jumped out at the sight of something exciting along the way. Some unthinking individuals tie the dog, probably not realizing that were he to jump under those circumstances, his neck would be broken, he could be dragged alongside the vehicle, or he could be hit by another vehicle. If for any reason you are taking your dog in an open-back

Opposite: A very sound Staffordshire Bull Terrier owned by Ellis and Faith Steinman.

233

truck, please have sufficient regard for that dog to at least provide a crate for him; and then remember that, in or out of a crate, a dog riding under the direct rays of the sun in hot weather can suffer and have his life endangered by the heat.

If you are staying at a hotel or motel with your dog, exercise him somewhere other than in the flower beds and parking lot of the property. People walking to and from their cars really are not thrilled at "stepping in something" left by your dog. Should an accident occur, pick it up with a tissue or paper towel and deposit it in a proper receptacle; do not just walk off, leaving it to remain there. Usually there are grassy areas on the sides of and behind motels where dogs can be exercised. Use them rather than the more conspicuous, usually carefully tended, front areas or those close to the rooms. If you are becoming a dog show enthusiast, you will eventually need an exercise pen to take

Cresstock Ode To Delight, a homebred owned by Bonnie Cresse of West Valley, UT, by Ch. Reetun's Red Tornado ex Ch. Cresstock Delight.

Ch. Athenian Angel placing Best of Breed at the prestigious Purina Invitational Dog Show in June, 1986. This outstanding SBT is the "winningest" bitch in the history of the breed, with Terrier Group placements to her credit. By Eng. Ch. Peg's Bolton Trip ex Kenwunn Supream, she was bred by Ian Chalk and is owned and handled by Joe LeBlanc.

with you to the show. Exercise pens are ideal to use when staying at motels, too, as they permit you to limit the dog's roaming space and to pick up after him more easily.

Never leave your dog unattended in the room of a motel unless you are absolutely certain that he will stay there quietly and not damage or destroy anything. You do not want a long list of complaints from irate guests, caused by the annoying barking or whining of a lonesome dog in strange surroundings, or an overzealous watch dog barking furiously each time a footstep passes the door or he hears a sound from an adjoining room. And you certainly do not want to return to torn curtains or bedspreads, soiled rugs, or other embarrassing evidence of the fact that your dog is not really house-reliable after all.

If yours is a dog accustomed to traveling with you and you are positive that his behavior will be acceptable when left alone, that is fine. But if the

Ch. Steinstaff Goin' For The Gusto, Am. and Can. C.D., winning his first leg on C.D., with a score of 181.5, in April, 1985. Mrs. Faith Steinman is the owner and handler.

slightest uncertainty exists, the wise course is to leave him in the car while you go to dinner or elsewhere; then bring him into the room when you are ready to retire for the night.

When you travel with a dog, it is often simpler to take along from home the food and water he will need rather than to buy food and look for water while you travel. In this way he will have the rations to which he is accustomed and which you know agree with him, and there will be no fear of problems due to different drinking water. Feeding on the road is quite easy now, at least for short trips, with all the splendid dry foods and high-quality canned meats available. A variety of lightweight, refillable water containers can be bought at many types of stores.

Always be careful to leave sufficient openings to ventilate your car when the dog will be alone in it. Remember that during the summer, the rays of

Top: No. 1 SBT Bitch in the nation for 1984 and a Group winner, Ch. Bullwatch Midnight Geisha was sired by Ch. Reetun's Lord Jim ex Ch. Starzend Midnight Gertie. Owner-handled by J. Zane Smith. *Bottom:* Am. and Can. Ch. Halsey's Black Eyed Susie, by Am. and Can. Ch. Sooner's Chocolate Teddy Bear ex Sooner's Merry Babe. A Top Producer, this splendid bitch has noted offspring to her credit. Photo courtesy of Lenna S. Hanna. Susie is pictured here with Olivia Parsons of the famed Sooner Kennels.

Right: Ch. WIN-R I'm A King Bee taking his third Terrier Group placement at age 19 months, under judge Mrs. Jane Forsyth. Owned by Judy Keller, Fort Collins, CO.

Below: Family portrait back in 1978. Left to right: Ch. Reetun's Lord Jim handled by J. Zane Smith; Ch. Piltdown Miss Equal handled by Lance Smith; and Ch. Reetun's Iron Duke handled by Rhett Smith. All are owned by J. Zane Smith.

the sun can make an inferno of a closed car within only a few minutes, so leave enough window space open to provide air circulation. Again, if your dog is in a crate, this can be done quite safely. The fact that you have left the car in a shady spot is not always a guarantee that you will find conditions the same when you return. Don't forget that the position of the sun changes in a matter of minutes, and the car you left nicely shaded half an hour ago

Left:
Ch. Sooner's Mistletoe, C.D.X., by Ch. Sooner's Captain Easy, was bred by Lois Smith and is owned by Elmer Parsons, who is handling her to this photographed win under judge Virginia Hampton.
Below:
Coalminer's Boy Minstrel, by Topcroft Minstrel Man ex Ch. Peck's Sexy Pants, pictured at age 11 months. Handled by Tracy Dineley for owner Alex Mudie, Canada. Bred by Mrs. Evelyn Frei.

can be getting full sunlight far more quickly than you may realize. So, if you leave a dog in the car, make sure there is sufficient ventilation and check back frequently to ascertain that all is well.

If you are going to another country, you will need a health certificate from your veterinarian for each dog you are taking with you, certifying that each has had rabies shots within the required time preceding your visit.

A Gallery of Historical Photos

Top: A really marvelous picture favored by the author, courtesy of John C. McCartney. *Bottom:* Actor Robert Newton, as Bill Sykes in the original film version of Dickens's *Oliver Twist,* casts a glance at his canine companion-actor, an SBT who plays Reylon Jake the Rake.

Top: This handsome portrait of Eng. Ch. Ben Hur was taken shortly after "Ben" won Best of Breed at the Easington-Peterlee Canine Society, County Durham, England, 1983. This important winning Staffordshire Bull Terrier was owned by Mr. R. Austin, Fenham, England. *Bottom:* Ch. Goldwyn's Leading Lad was behind many early Staffordshire Bull Terriers in the U.S. Note the soundness, ruggedness and type of this excellent dog. Photo courtesy of Joe LeBlanc.

Right: Ch. Rellun Fairyvale Victor, owned by Mrs. T. Miller, was a leading British winner in 1962. Photo by C.M Cook & Son Photographers, courtesy of Joe LeBlanc.

Below: Ch. Silverlake Iago (right), and his progeny for which he won the Stud Dog Class at a SBT Club Match in Seattle, WA.

242

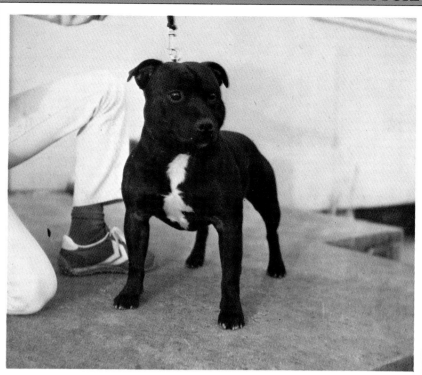

Left: Aust. Ch. Loggerhead's Penkridge at age two years. Imported from New Zealand, this dog has had an inestimable influence on the breed. *Below:* Note the magnificent body, legs, balance and structure of Ch. Rapparee Renegade. Bred by S. Bennett. Owned by Mr. and Mrs. J. Bolton.

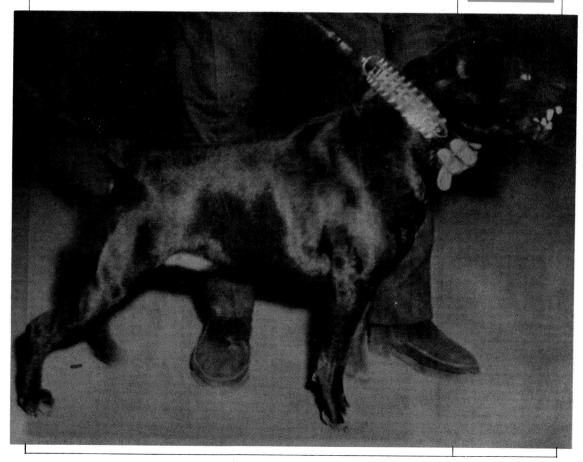

Top: This famous Stafford, Ch. Hyndland Jaunty Jock, was Best of Breed at Crufts in 1966. Photo courtesy of Joe LeBlanc.

Bottom: A dog of beautiful type and quality, Gamecock Another Brinsley Lad is a noted import from Great Britain and found in many American pedigrees. Photo courtesy of Joe LeBlanc.

English Ch. Curfews White Orchid, an extremely important member of the breed, was Best of Breed at Crufts in 1967. Photo courtesy of Joe LeBlanc.

Top: English breeder, judge and writer, Mr. A.W.A. "Nap" Cairns shown here working the 1974 Omaha Fun Match. The puppy is Kingsblood Royal Val, who won Best in Match, owner-handled by Dr. John H. Martin. *Bottom:* Reylon Jake the Rake. This SBT won considerable fame for himself and his breed in his performance as a canine film star. Photo courtesy of Joe LeBlanc.

Top: Ch. Silverzend Satan was Top Dog All Systems for his breed in 1975, 1976, and 1977; Top American-bred 1975 through 1978; and Top Stud Dog for his breed in America in 1979. His show wins include 67 times Best of Breed and 11 Group placements. *Bottom:* Eng. Ch. Topcroft Toreador was a dominant and important English sire and winner in the early 1970s. Photo courtesy of Joe LeBlanc.

Index

"Aahz", 39
Adam, Ann, 64
Agincourt Annie Oakley, Ch., 52
Airdstock Kate Kelly, Ch., 75
Airedale Terriers, 106
AKC Centennial 1984, 17, 222
AKC/UKC dual-registered, 23
Alan's Dynamo, Ch., 82
Allendale King, Ch., 57
Allen, John, 72
Almajon Stargazer, Ch., 69, 143
Altoft, J.A., 84
Ameretta and Cream, Ch., 42
American-bred Class, 164, 165, 168
American Bull Terrier, 9
American Kennel Club, 9, 10, 44, 46, 52, 66, 69, 95, 97, 113, 121, 161, 162, 168, 169, 178
— Address, 109
— Stud Book, 165
Amisano, Al, 14
Am Staff Club National Specialty, 29
Am Staffs in the U.S.A., 19–44
Angel Heart, 31
Angulation, 106
Apartments, 123
"April", 110
Aranda Angelina V. Kodiak, Ch., 30, 216
Aranda Kennels, 29
Archer's Muneca Dulsie De G's, C.D., Ch., 21
Arm-cards, 183
Associated Terrier Club 1986, 215
Athenian Angel, Ch., 56, 163, 235
Austin, Mr. and Mrs. R., 80
Baines, Peter, 20
Bald Eagle K.C. 1984, 30
Bandit's Brintiga, Ch., 51
Bar-Gray's Lucifer Sun, 65, 89
Barker, Linda, 44
Barker's Big City Slicker, Ch., 44, 227
Barker's Silverlake Lil, Ch., 44, 44
Barker's Staffordshire Bull Terriers, 44
Barker's Tank of Aramis, 44, 139
Barking, 123
Barnard, Jack, 77
Barway Chantilly Lace V. Aranda, 30
Barzak breeding, 64
Barzak Kennels, 50
Barzak's Lady Winifred, C.D., Ch., 64, 108
Barzak Staffords, 64
Barzak's Wild Jim, Ch., 66
Barzak's Wild Reginald, C.D., Ch., 64

Bathing, 159
Bayshire's Medallion, C.D., Ch., 198
Beagles, 57
Behavior patterns, 128
Beilby, H.N., 77
Belle, Ch., 104
Ben Hur, Ch., 80, 112, 241
Benoit, Kay A., 44, 65, 66, 67
Berrien Springs K.C. 1982, 181
Berry, D., 81
Best Brace, 174
Best Junior Handler, 175
Best of Breed, 170, 171, 174
Best of Opposite Sex, 170
Best of Variety, 170
Best of Winners, 170
Betchgreen Bargee, 73
Bethane Barney Bates, 88
Birmingham Championship Show 1985, 88
Biscuits, 150
Bite, exhibiting, 158
Biting, 124
Black and tan coloration, 105, 106
Black and Tan Terrier, 7
Blackcountry Kipper, Ch., 16
Black Tusker, Ch., 81, 88
Blue gene, 105
Blue Steel Alfredo Paiz, 45
Blue Steel Aretha, 45
Blue Steel Staffordshire Bull Terriers, 44–45
"Blueto", 92
Boam, Malcolm, 88
Boathouse Kennels, 82
Bobo's Gallant Gladiator, Ch., 66
Bolte, Damara, 15
Bones, 152
Boston Terrier, 7
Boswell, G. and M., 75, 76
Bottle feeding, 227
Brace Class, 174
Brave Nell, 77
Bred-by-Exhibitor Class, 164, 165, 168
Breech birth, 225
Breed standards, 97-103
Breeding, 199–231, 208–209, 214–215
Breeding program, 114
Breeding stock, 110
Bringarry Dangerman, Ch., 52, 53
Brisbin, I. Lehr, Vice President, 14
Brittany Brass Tacks, Ch., 75
Brittany Brazen Hussy, Ch., 76
Bronx County K.C.,
— 1979, 27
— 1983, 185, 205
Brood bitch, 202–208

Brood Bitch Class, 174
Brown, Carolyn, 24, 130
Brown, Dr. Jerry E., 20, 22
Brown, Hugh C., Jr., 20
Brown, Jim, 24, 131
Brown, Julianna A., 20, 22, 197, 228, 229
Brown, Patrick Julian, 194
Brown, Stacie Lee, 19
Brucellosis, 204
Buccaneer Shoemaker, Ch., 69
Buckland Staffords, 45–46
Bucks County K.C. 1986, 33
Bullbaiting, 7, 8
Bulldogs, 7, 46
Bullseye Abomindog, 44
Bullseye Double Rank, Ch., 50, 51, 102, 152
Bullseye Forget-Me-Not, Ch., 50, 160
Bullseye Kennels, 46–51
Bullseye Red Renegade, Ch., 9, 50, 56
Bull Terriers, 7, 37
Bullwatch Midnight Geisha, Ch., 50, 237
Bullwatch So Good of Starzend, Ch., 58
Byron's Finn McCool, Ch., 31, 41
Caesarean section, 226, 231
Cairns, A.W.A. "Nap", 81, 246
Calhoun, Dorene, 57
California National Specialty, 26
Call Me Katie Scarlet, Ch., 20, 166
Call Me Rhett Butler, Ch., 19, 20
Call Me Staffs Kennels, 19–20
Campbell, Art and Wanda, 29
Cardigan Welsh Corgis, 51
Carstaff Dancing Queen, Ch., 85
Casey, 158
C.D., 192
C.D.X., 192
Cerberus's Pecan Poko, Ch., 138
Chainmaker Amour Augusta, Ch., 16
Chainmaker Brazen Bomber, Ch., 16
Chainman Proteus, Ch., 86
Championship points, 164, 169
"Chantris", 37
Chapman, Mr. and Mrs., 84
Chapultepec Boy, 84
Charbert's Diamond Jim, Ch., 165
Chariff, Wayne M., 27, 28, 29
Chestonian Annoyance, Ch., 82
Chewing, 136, 150–155
Chicago Specialty 1982, 26
Chikako Black and White Tatoo, C.D., 197
Chikako I'm A Black Katoo, 197

249

Children, 123, 142
Circe Von Brown, Ch., 22
Clandara Kennels, 93
Clark, Anne, 188
Clark, Houston, 13, 14
Coalminer-Clandara Staffordshire
  Bull Terriers, 93
Coalminer's Blueberry Pie, Ch., 92,
  93
Coalminer's Boy Minstrel, Ch., 92,
  183, 239
Coalminer's I'm a Blueberry Too,
  162
Coalminer's Mystery Man, Ch., 92,
  207, 219
Coalminer's Red Rose, Ch., 91
Coalminer's Sadie Lady, 91
Coalminer Staffordshire Bull
  Terriers, 91
Coat conditioning, 158–159
Cock 'N' Bull Kennels, 20–22
Cock 'N' Bull's Blu Pauly, 197
Cock 'N' Bull's Poppycock, C.D.,
  Ch., 85, 197
Cockney Cracker, Ch., 66
Collars, 138
Commercial foods, 148
Companion Dog, 192
Companion Dog Excellent, 192
Conditioning, 157
Conqueror's Caesar, Ch., 16
Conqueror's Contessa, Ch., 16
Constable's Billy Club of Silverlake,
  Ch., 16, 52
Constipation, 153
Correia, Diane, 185
Craftwood Fancy, 17
Craighollows, Jean Short's, 57
Crates, 135–136, 204, 234
Crate training, 145, 160
Crawford, Cindy, 54
Cresstock Grand Slam, Ch., 150
Cresstock Hot Item, Ch., 201
Cresstock Kharisma, Ch., 84
Cresstock Logo of Linden, Ch., 161,
  170
Cresstock Necromancer, C.D., Ch.,
  45, 46, 195
Cresstock Ode To Delight Ch., 46,
  234
Cresstock Omega, Ch., 78
Cresstock Our Lady Goldberry, Ch.,
  45, 104, 226
Cresstock Our Tawny, Ch., 221
Cresstock's Delight, Ch., 46
Crossguns Annie Strong, Ch., 74
Crossguns Artful Dodger, 75
Crossguns Bravassa, Ch., 73, 74
Crossguns Johnson, 77
Crossguns Kennels, 73, 74
Crossguns Mr. Peggotty, 75
Crowe, Barry, 64
Crowe, Margaret, 50
Crowther, Betty, 10
Cruft's Show
— 1936, 77

— 1967, 245
— 1974, 47
— 1981, 84
— 1983, 85
— 1984, 85
"Crunch", 23, 36, 41
Crusader line, 33
Crusader's Cinderella, Ch., 14
Crusader's Gay Blade, Ch., 14
Cunningham, Mr., 85
Curfews White Orchid, Ch., 245
Dachshunds, 37, 41
"Dagmar", 28, 29, 126, 132, 167,
  172
Daktari Brutus, Ch., 72
Daktari Warchief, C.D.X., Ch., 45,
  72, 93
Dallas National Specialty 1984, 41
Dancinsun's Lord Gretsch, 200
Daniell-Jenkins, D., 228
Daniels, Bill, 16, 58, 60, 107
Daniels, Judi, 16, 17, 50, 54, 55, 58,
  60, 66
Darton of Henstaff, 58
Davenhill Kennels, 51–53
Davenhill's Adamant Angus, Ch.,
  51, 52
Davenhill's Firebrewed Brody, Ch.,
  52, 214
Davenhill's Rikki Tikki, Ch., 52,
  206
Davenhill's Silverlake Dawn, Ch.,
  52
Davenhill's Silverlake Lisa, Ch., 52,
  207
Davenhill's Silverlake Raven, Ch.,
  52, 53
Davenport, Daryl L., 51
Deadgame Assassin, 74
Deadgame Bossy Boots, 74
Deadgame Buck Rogers, Ch., 15, 74
Deadgame Canned Heat, Ch., 73,
  74
Deadgame Crimson Cloud, Ch., 73,
  74
Deadgame Double Dealer, Ch., 73,
  74
Deadgame Du Vienne, Ch., 73, 74
Deadgame Dynasty, 73
Deadgame Kingstown, 72
Deadgame Ned Kelly, Ch., 68, 74,
  75
Deadgame Nuclear Nell, Ch., 73
Deadgame Regae, 74
Deadgame Silk Degree, 74
Deadgame Staffordshire Bull
  Terriers, 72–75
Delaware Water Gap K.C. 1986,
  200, 204
Demon Seed, Ch., 104
Dennybeck Devil May Care, 84
Deno's Diamond of Steeltown, 22
Dental caries, 150
Desmond, Nigel, 26
"Desty", 65
Diamond Paladin, Ch., 25

Diamond Ringmaster of Evergreen,
  Ch., 25
Diamonds Crystal of Kar-Ron, Ch.,
  205
Diamonds Hot Wax of Sans Tache,
  Ch., 56, 129
Diamond's Paladin, Ch., 22
Dineley, Tracy, 78, 92, 93, 183, 239
Diseases, 150
Distemper, 150
Doberman Pinschers, 42, 105
Doc's Little Butch, Ch., 53
Doc's Little Fancy Lynn, Ch., 53
Doc's Little Grundoon, Ch., 53
Doc's Little Irate Irene, Ch., 53, 70,
  101
Doc's Little Irma, Ch., 53
Doc's Little Otis, 84
Doc's Staffordshire Bull Terriers,
  53–54
Dogfighting, 8, 9–10
Don Carlos Blu's Boomerang, Ch.,
  40
Dorffats Shanrick King, Ch., 75
Dragonquest and Nazan Kennels, 54
Dross, Jeanne Pierrette, 18, 54, 55,
  56, 116, 188, 189
Dry foods, 148
Dual-registered AKC/UKC, 23
Dunn, Joe, 77
"Dynamo", 54
Earle, George, 57
Eastaff Danom, Ch., 51
Eastaff Guardian, Ch., 89
Eastern Dog Club 1980, 126
Elder, Barbara, 54
Elvinor Miranda, 51
Emma of Gal, 85
English Springer Spaniels, 105
English Terrier, 7
Entries, 161, 164
Esteves, Nancy, 13
Esteves, Rudolph V., 13
Estrella's Valhalla Estrallita, C.D.,
  Ch., 16
Evans, Mark and Wendy, 75
Evastaff Kennels, 75–76
Evastaff Naughty Nell, 76
Evergreen American Staffordshire
  Terriers, 24–26, 130
Evergreen's Apache Belle, Ch., 25
Evergreen's Chicago Bear, Ch., 24,
  25
Evergreen's Demon Seed, C.D.,
  Ch., 24, 145
Evergreen's Earth Angel, Ch., 25
Evergreen's Midnight Lace, Ch., 20
Evergreen's Sundancer, Ch., 25
Exercise, 136, 137
Farmington K.C. 1975, 86
Farnsworth, Patricia A., 92
Feeding, 139–140, 147–150, 227–228
Feeding dishes, 138
Fencing, 122–123, 136–137, 138
Field Spaniels, 105
Fight Back, 52

Fighting, 122
Filmore Tuffy, Ch., 53
Firestaff No Scruples, Ch., 76
Flynn, Dennis J., 44, 45
Forester, Marion, 15, 57, 58, 72
Forsyth, Jane, 238
Fort Worth K.C. 1986, 45
Fox Terriers, 7, 106
Foy, Marcia, 173
Fraja Maria's Ace In The Hole, Ch., 30
Fraja Maria's Tia Maria, Ch., 29
Fraja's E.C. Dodge City, Ch., 154, 224
Fraja's Thunder Battery, Ch., 126, 172
Frampton, Tom, 200
Fraser, Jacqueline, 14, 29, 172
"Fred", 128
Frei, Evelyn, 91, 92, 93
Futurity Stakes, 174
Gait, 106, 159, 185, 186, 187
Gallant-Crusader line, 32
Gallant Kennels, 13
Gallant Kimbo R, Ch., 14
Gallant Pistol Pete, Ch., 14
Gallimore, Gwen, 57
Gallop, 186
Gamecock Another Brinsley Lad, Ch., 15, 16, 244
Gamecock Collector's Item, Ch., 16
Gamecock Dark Image, Ch., 16
Gamecock Hatchetman, Ch., 16
Gamecock Night Must Fall, Ch., 16
Gamecock The Great White Hope, Ch., 16
Gamecock Winter Shadow, Ch., 16
Game Lad, 77
Gamestar Vagabond, Ch., 69, 72
Gates, 138
Gentleman Jake the Red, 91
Gentleman Jim, Ch., 77
German Shorthaired Pointers, 57
Giles, Terry, 88
Ginnels Black Tuskyana, Ch., 88
Ginnels Maddonna's Moon Maid, Ch., 88
Glamour Girl, Ch., 11
Goddard, Debbie, 36
Golden Retrievers, 197
"Goldie", 46
Goldwyn Golden Lad, Ch., 88, 116
Goldwyn Leading Lad, Ch., 82, 241
Goldwyn Leading Star, Ch., 82, 84, 85
Goldwyn line, 84
Goldwyn Lucky Star, Ch., 85, 117
Great Britain, 69
Great Danes, 29, 30
Green, Frank, 55, 86
Gregory, Alan, 72, 73, 74
Grooming, 159
Grooming tools, 179
Guardstock's Red Atom, Ch., 6, 52, 56, 58, 59, 63, 64, 107

Guardstock's Samson Kenmore, Ch., 52, 71
Guardstock's Witches Double, Ch., 52, 196
Gumabone®, 155, 155
Gypsy Queen, 54
"Hacksaw", 231
Half and Halfs, 8
Halsey's Black Eyed Susie, Ch., 237
Hampton, Virginia, 239
Handlers, 161, 162
Handling, 159, 160
Hanna, Lenna S., 23, 34, 39
Harper, W.O., 13
Harrisburg K.C. 1985, 187
Harrison, Jack, 10
Harrison, Sharon, 10
Haus Trevilians Kennels, 23
Heathcliffe, C.D.X., 24
Heather's Brindle, C.D.X., 24
Heaton, Delphine, 197
Heaton, Ed, 197
Herk's Kizzy of Fraja, Ch., 30
Herring's Beau Jangles, Ch., 42, 43, 177
Herring's Red Ruby, 43
Hertfordshire Agriculture Society, 77
Hillstaff Iced Diamond, 84
Hogan, Florise, 26, 52, 53
Horowitz, David, 53
Hotels, 181, 234
House training, 113
Howard, Dean D., 11
Humane Society's Animal Facilitated Therapy Program, 22
Hunt, Paul R., 17, 180
Hyndland Jaunty Jock, Ch., 244
Idaho Capitol City K.C.
— 1983, 201
— 1985, 221
Immunizations, 145–146
Inbreeding, 208, 210
Inoculations, 229
Interbreeding, bulldogs, 7
Intermountain K. C., 1986, 226
International K. C. of Chicago, 11
Iron Buck's Painted Horse, Ch., 26, 27, 190
Iron Buck's Painted Tart, C.D., Ch., 27, 127
Iron Buck Staffordshire Terriers, 26–27
Izant, Edith, 9
"Jamie", 40
Jane's the Girl, 82
Jedediah of Cresstock, 96
Jefferies, John, 17
Jim the Dandy, 77
Johnny Walker, 137
Jolihem Battle Flame, 82
Jolihem Dreadnaught, Ch., 82
Jolihem El Toro, Ch., 82
Jolihem Wicked Lady, 82
Jones, Tony, 88

Judael strain, 57
Judy of Jolihan, Ch., 85
Junior Class, 175
Junior Showmanship, 174–175, 178
Kalamazoo K.C. 1986, 174
Kalliope's Autumn Nocturne, 56
Kalliope's El Torito Rojo, Ch., 51
Kalliope's Faust, Ch., 16
Ka Nakht Jack O'Diamonds, Ch., 54, 210
Ka Nakht Moss Rose, 54, 210
Kar-Ron's Crystals Lil' Engorcer, Ch., 218
Kar-Ron's Finwar's Solace, Ch., 187
Kar-Ron's Finwar's Success, 204
Kar-Ron's Gentleman Jim, Ch., 146
Kar-Ron's John Henry, 230
Kar-Ron's Komet of Ledge Rock, 215
Kavalier's Lord Jeff, Ch., 16
"Kea", 110
Keenan, Barbara, 172
Keller, Judy, 64
Kennel Club of Great Britain, 7, 8, 10, 80
Kennel stock, 120
Kentucky National Specialty 1980, 28
Keystone Beauregard, 45
Kinderlee Clanaboy, 82
Kinder's Blue at WildWind, Ch., 43, 193
Kingsblood Royal Val, Ch., 16, 52, 53, 128, 246
"Kirk", 28
Kirkee American Staffordshire Terriers, 27–29
Kirkee's Polar Bear of Fraja, C.D., Ch., 29, 169
Kirk's Daughter O'The Regiment, Ch., 29
Klinckhardt, Emil, 78
Kodiak Kennels, 29–32
Kodiak's Blaque Jaque, Ch., 30, 31, 32
Kodiak's Blue Haze, Ch., 31, 209
Kodiak's Kare Bear, Ch., 31
Kodiak's Rhythm in Blue, 31, 32
Kodiak's The Joker's Wild, Ch., 31
Kodiak's Tina Turner Review, 31
Kodiak's Windrider, 31, 127
Koehler, Dick, 197
"Korny", 24
Krohne, Ron, 32, 89, 138
Kuberski, Michele, 231
Kurnpow Pied Piper, 75
Labrador Retrievers, 57
Ladies and Gentlemen, 88
Lady Barzak's Lady Winfred, Ch., 115
Lady Eve, Ch., 77
Lamont, Sid, 23
Lanreen Candy May, 91, 92
Latham, Harry, 81
Lead training, 143
LeBlanc, Cheryl, 56, 57, 58

LeBlanc, Joe, 56, 57, 58, 59, 210, 235
Ledge Rock American Staffordshire Terriers, 32–34
Ledge Rock's Blue Velvet, 131
Ledge Rock's Buckeye Velvet, Ch., 34, 192, 212
Ledge Rock's Cherokee Fiddler, 134, 144
Ledge Rock's Kopper Korn, Ch., 32, 33, 132, 159, 164, 166, 222
Ledge Rock's Lucy In The Sky, Ch., 34, 132, 179
Ledge Rock's Rucky Velvet, Ch., 162
Ledge Rock's Sweet Potatoe, Ch., 33
Lee, Nancy, 54
Legs, 192
Leoline Gallant Hussar, 181
Leoline Little Lady, 53
Linebreeding, 208, 210
"Little Red", 192
Liver coloration, 105, 106
Liversidge, Mrs. , 10
Lloyd, Charles, President, 14
Lochner, Tom and Shelly, 53
Lochness Lonnie McBlue, Ch., 92
Lochness Ravoona Lady, Ch., 53
Lochness Ravoon Buster, Ch., 17, 53, 54, 180
Logan's Cock O'The Walk, Ch., 52
Logan's Jack Thrasher, Ch., 52, 52
Logan's Molly Thrasher, Ch., 52
Logansport K.C. 1984, 54
Loggerhead Kennels, 16, 72
Loggerhead's Boolarra, Ch., 72
Loggerhead's Filanda, Ch., 58
Loggerhead's Gaylord, Ch., 210
Loggerhead's Helle, Ch., 72
Loggerhead's Jim Crow, Ch., 72
Loggerhead's, Marion Forester's, 57
Loggerhead's Nekron, Ch., 72
Loggerhead's Penkridge, Ch., 73, 74, 76, 243
Loggerhead's Pensnett, Ch., 69
Loving, Douglas K., 23, 41
Lucarelli, Joe, 34
Lucarelli, Joye, 34
Lucarelli Kennels, 34
Lucas Cool Hand Luke, Ch., 29
Lydick, Dr. Eva, 31
Lymstaff Lady Flash of Zabarette, 85
McCartney, John C., 27, 28, 29, 126, 151, 154, 167, 172, 224
McKenney, Dick, 65, 89
"Maestro", 207
Maher's Captain D, Ch., 11
Major in Command of Wychbury, Ch., 82
Malaser Mauler, Ch., 85
Mallen, Joe, 77
Malstaffs Proud Becky, 88
Manchester Terriers, 7, 105
Marabank Diamond Lil, Ch., 72

Mari-Don Kirkee Battery, Ch., 27, 28, 29
Marion Forester Memorial Trophy, 72
Marsh, Jerri, 53
Marsh, Phil, 62
Martin, Dr. John H., 50, 53, 54, 70, 105, 181, 246
Marushak, Fred J. and Sharon A., 29, 30, 31
Marusich, Kathleen, 11
Marusich, Oscar, 11
Mary Poppins, 82
Masebo's Awesome Alice 17, 53
Massey, J. David, 17, 181
Match shows, 160–161
Media, 123, 125
Merle, 24
Merritt, Dana, 16
Merritt, Jenny, 16
Metro Goldwyn Mayer Studios, 23
Michelson, Timothy F., 45, 72, 93
Millgarth Powerpack, C.D., Ch., 16, 17, 47, 53
Miscellaneous Class, 15
Mississippi Coast K.C. 1986, 89
Mitchell, Don, 72
Moberly K.C. 1986, 56
Montgomery County K.C.
— 1979, 28
— 1981, 29
— 1985, 42, 209
Moore, Annemarie, 41
Morely, Bill, 57
Mother Lode Gypsophila, Ch., 44, 45, 225
"Motley", 112
Mountainash Christmas Aray, Ch., 72
Mountainash Xmas Ajax, Ch., 72
Mount Shires I'm a Wheezer, Ch., 24
Mudie, Alex, 92
Naming your dog, 143
National Specialty 1983, 27
National Specialty, 1984, 34
National Specialty, Am Staff, 1975, 125
Nazan's Double Dynamo, Ch., 54, 55
New Brunswick K.C., 138
New South Wales Championship Stafford Show 1986, 76
New South Wales Staffordshire Bull Terrier Show 1980, 73
Newton K.C. 1985, 41
Newton, Robert, 240
Nicholas, Anna K., 133, 185, 189, 200, 205, 224
Nitemarch Petite Miss, Ch., 75
No. 1 SBT Bitch, U.S.
— 1982, 50, 221
— 1984, 44, 57, 237
No. 1 SBT, Canada, 1986, 92
No. 3 SBT, Canada, 1979, 47
No. 3 SBT Dog, U.S., 1980, 55

No. 3 SBT, U.S.,
— 1984, 44
— 1985, 50
No. 5 Am Staff, U.S., 1986, 19
No. 7 SBT Dog U.S., 1979, 55
Non-regular Class, 171, 174
Normandie Ides of March, Ch., 55, 185, 188
Normandie Lady of Shars, Ch., 56, 116
Normandie Staffordshire Bull Terriers, 18, 54–56
Northeastern IN K.C. 1984, 61
Northeastern SBT Club, 80
Northern Counties (1943), 77
Northwark Becky Sharp, Ch., 15, 16, 58
Northwark Joyous, Ch., 69
Northwark Silverlake, Ch., 66
Northwest Staffordshire Bull Terrier Club, 77
Norton, Mark, 81
Norton, T.A., 80, 81
Novice Class, 164–165, 168
Novice Junior Showmanship, 175
Nugent's Merry Midnight, C.D., Ch., 37, 39
Nutmeg Force Majeure, Ch., 16
Nylabone®, 138, 154, 155
Nylon bones, 153
Obedience, 191–197
Obedience Trial Champion, 192
Obedience trials, 191–192
Old Dominion K.C. 1985, 19
Oltyme's Cock O' The Walk, Ch., 95, 153, 229
Omaha Fun Match 1974, 246
Open Class, 164, 165, 167, 168
Open Junior Showmanship, 175
Orchid Challenger, 54
Ormsby, Clifford A., 11
O.T.Ch., 192–193
Our Gang, 128
Outcrossing, 208, 210
Owning A Staffordshire, 122–125
Paignton Championship Show 1985, 88
Paper training, 144–145
Parsons, Elmer, 37, 38, 172, 239
Parsons, Olivia, 237
Pasadena K.C. 1986, 54, 55
Patterson, Olivia, 37, 38, 40, 125, 230
Patterson, Wayne, 37
"Patton", 18, 55
Patton breeding, 22
Patton's Smoki Topaz, Ch., 119
Patton's Texas Belle Lucy, Ch., 21
Patton's White Rock Penny, Ch., 21
Peck's Pimpernel of Stonefort, Ch., 52
Peck's Sexy Pants, Ch., 78, 92
Peck's Toshia Luckey, Ch., 52
Pedigree, 120, 204, 208
Penn Treaty K.C.
— 1985, 218

— 1986, 230
Pens, 180, 183
Pepper Ridge Fraja's Thunder Battery, Ch., 28
Peta the Bomber, 82
"Pete", 128
Petting, 123
Phillips, Robert W., 51
Pick of the litter, 217
"Piggie", 45
Piltdown Bill of Truestaff, Ch., 44
Piltdown Keltic Druid, Ch., 18, 50, 54, 189
Piltdown Kennels, 17, 47
Piltdown line, 51
Piltdown Mata Hari, Ch., 50, 70, 221
Piltdown Miss Equal, Ch., 47, 50, 238
Piltdown Red Contessa, Ch., 16, 47
Piltdown St. Eve, 18, 50, 55
Piske, Mae, 26
Pit Bull Terriers, 8, 9, 20, 23, 57, 61, 123
Pit dogs, 8
Pitshaft Wiseguy, 72
Play, 136
Pocono Mountain K.C. 1985, 31
Pointers, 105
Point shows, 161–174
"Pookie", 163
Pooper Scoopers, 180
Potteries SBT Club 21st Anniversary Show, 88
Pregnancy, 202, 206–207, 220–231
Prehn, Ernest and Ruth, 32, 33, 34, 110, 222
Priffdinas Petrina, 52
Pringle, Ed, 57
Professional handlers, 110
Protection dogs, 122
Pugh, Mr. and Mrs., 84
Pumptail Dragonstar Dancer, U.D., C.D.X., Can. C.D., Ch., 60, 61, 62, 63, 69, 78, 186, 194, 195
Pumptail Excalibur Essie, 45
Pumptail Staffordshires, 72
Pumptail Stardancer, Ch., 61, 69
Puppies, 110–112, 114, 118–119, 121, 135, 143, 203, 208, 213, 223–231
— Bringing home, 141–142
— Feeding, 149
Puppy Class, 162–164, 168
Puppy mills, 53
Puppy teeth, 150
Pure-Bred Dogs/American Kennel Gazette, 169, 170
Purina Invitational 1986, 235
Queen Bodicea, 82
Queenie, 77
Quo Vadis, 80
Ragtime Bombasto, Ch., 16
"Rambo", 168
Rannvan's Pride of Rannoch, Ch., 44, 50
Rant, Larry, 10

Rant, Lilian, 10
Rapparee bloodlines, 54
Rapparee Renegade, Ch., 243
Rapparee Rothersyke Vow, Ch., 69
Rawhide, 153
Rebel's Jess R, 14
Red Polly of Salken, Ch., 16, 17
Red Rock of Har-Wyn, Ch., 34
Red Ru, Ch., 84
Reetun's Aristocrat, Ch., 51
Reetun's Buffalo Bill, Ch., 51
Reetun's Iron Duke, Ch., 50, 51, 238
Reetun's Iron Magic, Ch., 50
Reetun's Iron Maiden, Ch., 50, 51
Reetun's Lord Jim, Ch., , 18, 47, 51, 55, 62, 133, 228, 238
Reetun's Red Tornado, Ch., 45, 50, 51
Reetun's Rufus The Red, Ch., 44, 50, 51, 83, 99, 100, 202
Reetun's Staffordshires, 47, 51
Register, Levon C., 14
Registration, 121–122, 162
Rehil, A., 32
Rellun Fairyvale, Ch., 242
Rendorn Drummer Boy of Razemick, Ch., 79
Reylon Jake the Rake, 240, 246
Reynolds, James G., 15
Rhody's Amstafs, 42
Richards, Kriss and Lorraine, 45, 46
Ringo, Ch., 104
Ringold, E.D., 14
Rio Grande K.C. 1981, 93
Rio Hondo K.C. 1986, 229
Rip Rock Golden Rock, Ch., 11
Rip Rock Irish Mike, Ch., 11
Rip Rock Silver Cavalier, Ch., 11
Roaming, 122, 125
Roberts, Kaye M., 19, 20
Rocellio Belle Star, 84
Rocellio Captain Morgan, 75, 76
Rocellio Miss Scarlett, 84
Rocellio Miss Supreme, 84
Rocky Mountain Ogre's Runnaway, Ch., 26
Rocky Mountain Tosca, Ch., 25
Rodgers, Chet, 42, 43
Rodgers, Chet III, 142
Rogers, Lauraine, 42, 43
Roll, Dr. Carroll A., 11
Roses are Red, 111
Rothersyke Jaunty Jake, 86
Rottweilers, 23, 36, 40
Rowdytown Jazz of Ledge Rock, Ch., 34
Rowe, Trevor, 88
Rowland, Dennis, 45
Rowland, Edward, 17, 47, 55
Rowland, Stella, 17
Ruffian Hercules of Har-Wyn, Ch., 21, 24
Ruffian Kennels, 13
Ruffian lady of Har-Wyn, Ch., 24

Ruffian line, 24, 26, 33
Ruffian Red Rock of Har-Wyn, Ch., 13, 14, 19
Ruffian Sky Bolt of Har-Wyn, Ch., 13, 24
Rumble, Stephen, 88
Ryan's D.J., Ch., 129, 151
Ryan's Hot Stuff, Ch., 167
Salken Resolute, 17
Sand and Sea K. C. Dog Show 1979, 28
Sans Tache's El Chivato, Ch., 17, 223
Sans Tache Staffordshire Bull Terriers, 56–57
Saw Mill K.C. 1986, 231
SBT Club Championship Show 1983, 80
Scalliwag of Cresstock, 114
Scariato, April, 130
Scariato, Daniel and Pamela, 128–129, 130
Scariato, Nick, 130
Schutzhund, 23
Scottsdale K.C. 1980, 160
Scratchline Staffords, 75
Season, bitch's, 113
Selwood, Steve, 158
Senior Class, 175
Shadoplay Dark Destiny, Ch., 65, 66
"Shady", 131
Shady Lady, 24, 25
Shalley, Lynn, 45
Shampoo, 159
Shea, Mike, 11, 20, 172
Shipping dogs, 111, 204-205
Shorrock, Joyce, 70, 81
Shortblok Zoril, 65
Short, Jean, 57
Shots, 141, 145–146, 229
Show, enjoyment of, 183–187
Show preparations, 178–183
Silverlake Diablo, Ch., 65
Silverlake Gemstock, Ch., 16, 51
Silverlake Gypsy Queen, Ch., 16, 54
Silverlake Hurricane, 46
Silverlake Iago, Ch., 44, 66, 67, 242
Silverzend Satan, Ch., 16, 51, 52, 247
Sindelar, Fred, 129
Sindelar's Doctor Mudd, Ch., 19, 20
S. Indiana SBT Club, September 1984, 17
Singleton, Jim, 45
Sir Vessa, Ch., 30
Sliverlake Dreadnought, Ch., 16
Smith, J. Zane, 9, 44, 46, 47, 50, 51, 62, 100, 102, 133, 160, 221, 228, 237, 238
Smith, Lance, 238
Smith, Lois, 38, 42
Smith, Rhett, 238
S'N'S Firehawk, 63
S'N'S Ogre Easy, Ch., 23, 36, 41, 156, 173

S'N'S Staffs, 23, 34
Socialization and Training, 142–146, 158
Solitaire of Topcroft, 81
Sooner breeding, 22
Sooner Kennels, 37, 38, 42
Sooner's Big Mac, Ch., 12
Sooner's Black Pepper, Ch., 34
Sooner's Boomer Sooner, Ch., 125
Sooner's Cherokee Strip, Ch., 217, 220
Sooner's Chocolate Teddy Bear, Ch., 37, 40
Sooner's Dr. Pepper, Ch., 13, 39, 172
Sooner's Flying Sorceress, Ch., 37, 39
Sooner's Fudge Ripple, 23, 40
Sooner's Lady Love, Ch., 35, 120
Sooner's Mac Attack, 118
Sooner's Mistletoe, Ch., 239
Sooner's Oklahoma Pride, Ch., 23, 41
Sooner's Our Man Flint, Ch., 39, 230
Sooner's Perfectly Demonic, Ch., 39, 141
Sooner's Rags to Riches, 40
Sooner's Ranger El Cajohn, Ch., 37
Sooner's Ranger El Capitan, Ch., 39
Sooner's Ring of Success, 37
Sooner's Shade Midnight, Ch., 38
Sooner's Steamboat Annie, Ch., 39
Sooner's True Grit of Rhody, Ch., 42
Southern Counties
— (1937), 77
— Championship Show 1985, 88
— SBT Society, 80
South Wales Championship SBT Club Specialty 1985, 88
Sparks, John, 23, 34
Spaying, 113
Specials, 170
Specialty, 174
Sporting dogs, 196
Stacking, 159, 185
Staff McMichael, Ch., 69, 73
Staffordshire Bull Terrier breed standard, 97–100
Staffordshire Bull Terrier British breed standard, 102–103
Staffordshire Bull Terrier British breed standard, 1935, 100–102
Staffordshire Bull Terrier Club, 54
Staffordshire Bull Terrier Club of America, 18
Staffordshire Bull Terrier Club of Northern New Jersey, 55
Staffordshire Bull Terrier Club of the U.S., 10
Staffordshire Bull Terrier Club, 77
Staffordshire Bull Terriers in the U.S.A., 44–67
Staffordshire Terrier breed standard, 95–97

Staffordshire Terrier Club of America, 10, 11, 14
Staff Status, 18
Stafwright Blake, Ch., 76
Standards, breed, 12–13, 97-103
"Star", 208
Star Prize, 84
Starved Rock K.C. 1986, 210
Starzend Becky Sharp, Ch., 69
Starzend Deacon, Ch., 16, 58
Starzend Faultless, Ch., 16, 58
Starzend Fred Again, Ch., 16, 58
Starzend Headliner, Ch., 16, 58
Starzend Isadora, Ch., 16, 58
Starzend Ivan The Red, Ch., 58
Starzend Jimdandy, Ch., 58
Starzend Kaptain Kirk, Ch., 58
Starzend Kennels, 16, 58-60
Starzend King's Crystal, C.D.X., Ch., 58
Starzend Martian Master, Ch., 52
Starzend Midnight Gertie, Ch., 58
Starzend Moondust, Ch., 52, 58
Starzend Satan's Mistress, Ch., 52, 58
Starzend Taurus, Ch., 58
Starzend Waltzing Matilda, Ch., 52, 58
Starzend Wonder Witch, Ch., 52
Starzend Zodiac Force, 51
Steeltown's Almost an Angel, C.D., Ch., 197
Steeltown's Blue Monday, Ch., 11, 20–21, 22, 97, 98, 122, 172, 192, 194
Steeltown's Diamond Boy, Ch., 197
Steeltown's Fancy Me Blue, 228
Steinman, Ellis and Faith, 60, 61, 62, 63
Steinman, Faith, 59, 78, 186, 193, 236
Steinstaff Goin' For The Gusto, C.D.X., T.D., Ch., 61, 63, 90, 174, 236
Steinstaff Staffordshire Bull Terriers, 60–64
Stevenson, Ann, 58
Stewards, 183
Stinson, I.N., 14
Stowe, Steve, 10
Strand, Ed, 58
Strathstaff Aggressor, 60
Stud Book registry, 8–9
Stud dog, 121, 203, 208–220, 213, 214
Stud Dog Class, 174
Stud fee, 203, 214–217
Sunny, Ch., 104
Sunrise Black Rose, 85
Superintendent, 162, 165
Supplements, food, 140
Sussex Spaniels, 105
Sweepstakes, 174
Sword and Sorcery American Staffordshire Terriers, 34–41

Sydney Royal Easter Show 73, 74, 75, 76
Symtan Striker, 53
Talk A Blue Streak, 130
Tara's Doc Holliday, Ch., 19, 20
Tara's Gingerbread Tart, Ch., 27
Tara's Muddi Fields Forever, Ch., 19, 182
Taylor, R. William, 28
Taylor, Tommy, 88
T.D., 193
T.D.X., 193
Teal, Mike, 197
Teal, Tami, 197
Team Class, 174
Temperament, 157
Terre Haute K.C. 1985, 64
Terrier Group, 12, 14
Texas Staffordshire Club, 41
Texsraff Royal Jester, Ch., 16
The Malaser Mauler, Ch., 85
Therapy dogs, 129
Thompson, William, 215
"Tie", 219
Tiger Crusader, Ch., 14
Tinkinswood Imperial, Ch., 16, 66
Titan's Roho Grande, Ch., 26
Tomlinson, Mrs., 85
Tondoo Forget Me Not, 89
Tondoo Guardian Angel, 89
Tondoo Hooker, 89
Tondoo Miss Moonshine, Ch., 88, 89
Tondoo Staffordshire Bull Terriers, 88–89
Tondoo Taboo, 89
Tondoo War Squaw, 89
Tooby, Mr. and Mrs., 85
Tooth decay, 150
Top American-bred 1975–1978, 52
Top Bitch, Am Staff, 1983, 16
Topcroft Benita, Ch., 82
Topcroft Kennels, 91
Topcroft Minstrel, 91, 92
Topcroft Toreador, Ch., 247
Topcroft Trailblazer, Ch., 80, 81
Top Dog All Systems 1975, 76, 77, 247
Top Dog, Am Staff, 1983, 16
Top Dog, SBT Club of America, 1975–1977, 16
Top Dog, SBT, U.S., 1975, 1976, 1977, 52
Top Producer 1984, 26
Top SBT Bitch U.S., 1985, 57
Top SBT, England, 1974, 47
Top SBT, England, 1985, 88
Top SBT Stud Dog U.S, 1979, 52, 247
Top SBT Stud Dog, U.S., 1980, 47
Top SBT, U.S., 1978, 47
Top SBT, U.S., 1979, 47
Top SBT, U.S., 1982, 54
Topstaff Willywood Goldy, 24
Topsy's Ghost, Ch., 11
Top Ten Am Staff 1984, 26

Top Ten Am Staff 1985, 26
Tracking Dog, 193
Tracking Dog Excellent, 193
Trail Creek Dog Training Club, 61
Training, 159, 191–197, 233
Training and Socialization, 142–146
Traveling, 146, 233–239
Travwall Breeders Dream, 82, 84
Travwall El Cid, Ch., 82
Treats, 157
Tricolors, 105
True Grit Cisco of Sligo, Ch., 178
Truestaff Orchid Challenger, Ch., 54
Trugrip Cotton Futures, Ch., 52
Trugrip Hagar of Val Verde, Ch., 67
Trugrip Horatio Hornblower, Ch., 16
Trugrip Jezebel, Ch., 16
Trugrip Kennels, 16
Trugrip Pendragon Red, Ch., 16
Trugrip Saxon, Ch., 67
Trugrip Seattle Sue, 67
Tryarr Blue Diamond, Ch., 22
Tryarr Diamondback Redbolt, Ch., 13, 22, 24, 25, 126, 132
Tryarr Diamonds Are Forever, Ch., 25
Tryarr Kennels, 13
Tryarr Strawberry Fields, Ch., 19
Tuskalear Broad Boy, 76
Tuskalear Staffordshire Bull Terriers, 76
Tuskalear Tunza`Strife, Ch., 75
Tuxedo Park K.C. 1984, 224
U.D., 192
United American Staffordshire Terrier Club Obedience Team, 197
United Kennel Club, 9, 23, 43, 44, 61
United States, Am Staffs in, 19-44
Utility Dog, 192
Val Verde Ababa, Ch., 44, 66
Val Verde, Ch., 184
Val Verde Cockney Cracker, Ch., 44, 88
Val Verde Dapper Diplomat, 66
Val Verde Eureka, 66, 67

Val Verde Gentry, Ch., 67
Val Verde Gidgit, Ch., 67
Val Verde Hesione, Ch., 67
Val Verde Staffordshire Bull Terriers, 65–67
Variety Group, 170, 171
Venable, Dan, 10
Venable, Judy, 10
Veterans Class, 174
Veterinarians, 140, 159
Victoria Golden Jubilee Championship Stafford Show 1985, 76
Violets Are Blue, 124
Virginia State Police Department Canine Program, 23
Vitamins, 147, 148
Wall, Alwyn, 82
Wall, Sheila and Peter, 81, 82, 84, 85, 88
Ward, Mr. and Mrs., 85
Water dishes, 138
Waters, Alex, 88
Wawocan Wundebar, 82
Weamera Cyclone, Ch., 72
Wellwisher of Wystaff, Ch., 69, 72
Westchester K.C.
— 1979, 27, 28
— 1980, 28, 29
— 1981, 29
— 1982, 167
— 1987, 20
West Riding Alfalfa, 58
Westwood, Jean, 88
Whalley, R., 75
What A Classy Chasis, Ch., 139
Wheat, James and Barbara, 26
Wheeler's Black Dinah, Ch., 11
"Wheezer", 130, 131
Wheezer's Shady Lady, 24, 104
Whelping, 223–226, 231
White Rock Dusty of Steeltown, Ch., , 21, 22
White Rock Grover, 21
White Rock Jet Bomber, Ch., 21
Wick, Eddie, 134
Wildfire, 139
Wildside Triple Truble, Ch., 76

WildWind Farm, 42–43
WildWind's Amy Tequila, Ch., 14
WildWind's Apache Brave, Ch., 42, 132
WildWind's Arabian Knight, Ch., 18
WildWind's Bella Donna, 121
WildWind's Butch Cassidy, 121
WildWind's Day Dream Fantasy, 103
WildWind's Fan Tom Of The Oprai, 43
WildWind's Midnight Revenge, C.D., U.D., Ch., 42, 142
WildWind's Sweet Chevron, Ch., 132
Williams, Claude, 15
Willie Mark's Miss Orday, 45, 192
Wills, 200–202
Willynwood Ogre's Angel, 24
Willynwood Velvet Shadow, C.D., Ch., 32, 136, 213
Windham County K.C. 1985, 165, 167
Windsor Championship Show 1985, 88
Winners Bitch, 168, 170, 171
Winners Class, 168–170
Winners Dog, 168, 170, 171
WIN-R's I'm A King Bee, Ch., 64, 238
WIN-R Staffordshire Bull Terriers, 64–65
Wood, Albert, 47, 51
Wormings, 141
Worms, 229
Wornall, Wood, 133
Wystaffs, 57
Wystaff Witchcraft, 58
Wystaff Worthy, Ch., 73
Wystall Warlock, Ch., 16
X-Pert Brindle Biff, Ch., 11
X-Pert Kennels, 13
X-Pert Morgan Romsy, Ch., 42
X-Pert Pedro Escopeta, Ch., 11
Yankee Terrier, 9
Yegans Lad, Ch., 72
Y-Ram Lad Alice, Ch., 16